Lord, I Have a Question

**Everything you ever wanted to ask God
but were afraid to say out loud**

DAN SMITH

Pacific Press® Publishing Association
Nampa, Idaho
Oshawa, Ontario, Canada
www.pacificpress.com

Designed by Dennis Ferree
Cover photo by Bob Thomas/Getty Images ©

Unless otherwise noted, all Scripture quotations
are from the New International Version.

Additional copies of this book are available by calling toll free 1-800-765-6955 or
visiting http://www.adventistbookcenter.com.

Library of Congress Cataloging-in-Publication Data

Smith, Dan, 1953-
Lord I have a question : everything you ever wanted to ask God
but were afraid to say out loud/Dan Smith.
p. cm.
Includes bibliographical references.
ISBN: 0-8163-2016-0
1. Apologetics. I. Title

BT1103.S632004
230'.6732—dc22   2003070664

04 05 06 07 08 • 5 4 3 2 1

Dedication

I dedicate this, my first and maybe only book(!), to my wife Hilda, who, when some new ideas about God first excited me back when we were dating, said, "But that's what I've been trying to tell you for the past eighteen months!" And to our two sons, Alex and Eric. And to my father, D. K. Smith, who passed away last year and with whom for forty-nine years I shared a love for the church, for pastoring, and for thinking about God.

Table of Contents

Preface

I send this book into the world gingerly, wishing it were better, wanting to rewrite it again! Every week that I preach, I see something more clearly, find something I wish I could have added. A printed book crystallizes a particular moment in one's theological journey—and fossilizes that moment. I send this book out with a prayer that it will bless, that it will make more friends for God, and that I have "spoken what is right" about God (Job 42:8).

I've done the best I can to root every thought in inspired writings. If you find areas of my thinking that need to be revised or need greater clarity, I will try to receive your suggestions with grace and respect. Our church has a Web site, www.lsuchurch.org, where you can communicate with me. Persuade me of greater truth and I'll keep on revising until we can walk through the gates and see and hear ultimate Truth Himself face to face!

I want to thank the people whose ideas have given me pieces of this puzzle of a picture of God that I've put together: (in alphabetical order) Fritz Guy, Hans LaRondelle, C. S. Lewis, Graham Maxwell, Keith Miller, Jack Provonsha, Smuts van Rooyen, Stuart Tyner, my Venden family, Dick Winn, Philip Yancey, and hundreds of other friends, church members, and fellow pastors in books, tapes, and conversations over Sabbath dinners and around campfires at the beach.

Preface

I also want to thank Jenni Subriar, my assistant, who spent untold unpaid hours helping get the details right. And I owe deep appreciation to the Southeastern California Conference, to my La Sierra University Church, and to our pastoral staff for a brief sabbatical this past year during which I hammered out a rough draft. Otherwise this book comes out of a regular pastor's life and preaching—a pastor whose life mission is to discover God's goodness and to communicate that goodness to people.

CHAPTER ONE

Why Even Ask Questions About God?

I heard Chuck Colson tell a story once about the time he had the opportunity to speak at the Marine Academy, his alma mater. He gave his message to thousands of cadets, with all the Academy brass sitting on the front row, resplendent in their dress uniforms and medals. At the end, Colson asked if there were any questions. There was a long silence. Then the six-foot-six-inch superintendent stood up, turned to the cadets, and said firmly, *"There* will *be questions!"*

I have questions—questions such as why did Jesus have to die? Why in the world does God allow so much suffering? Why doesn't God answer more prayers, do more miracles today? And what about all the hard stories in the Old Testament? I don't know about you, but I've never been able to put these questions and others like them on the shelf and keep them there for very long. I was born asking questions.

Shortly after I began dating Hilda, who's now my wife, I showed up to celebrate her birthday and noticed that someone else had sent flowers to her. Repressing some jealous fears, I asked, "Who are the flowers from?" I couldn't go out to eat—I couldn't do anything— until I had my question answered. She assured me that I had nothing to worry about. And when I had that answer, I could let the relationship move forward!

It's been the same for me—and millions of others—with God: We can live with some questions, but we can't put them *all* on the shelf. Some keep our relationship with God from moving forward.

I think my questions started with prayer. Right after I graduated from college, I was assigned to a series of tent meetings in Portland, Oregon. Almost no one was coming, and so the series' staff held many prayer sessions during which they begged God to bless our meetings by sending people. Eventually, I couldn't resist asking, "Do we really expect God to force people to come against their will? Wasn't God already trying His hardest to persuade people to come? If our prayers helped some to get saved, what about those who didn't have anyone praying for them? Does prayer really work, and if so, how?"

No one appreciated my questions very much, but I was absolutely serious.

Then, as I read through the Bible, I couldn't help but get stuck with some of the hard questions in the Old Testament (and in the New):

> *Where is the love of God in all this?*
> *Why did God have to kill Uzzah just for trying to keep the ark from falling over?*
> *Why did God have to turn Lot's wife into a pillar of salt just for looking back once?*
> *When God punished people, did He really have to kill all the women and children too?*
> *When He gave the Ten Commandments, was it really necessary for Him to shout and to use thunder, smoke, and fire?*
> *What about Ananias and Sapphira dropping dead just because they held back some money?*
> *And what about the smoke of the sinners' torment ascending day and night for ever and ever?*

Why Even Ask Questions About God?

Then, pastoring at Newbury Park Academy, I found myself wrestling with questions about the Cross:

> *Why did Jesus have to die?*
> *Why does the forgiveness of sins require blood? Jesus tells us to forgive, to turn the other cheek—why didn't God forgive without requiring someone to die?*
> *How does the death of one person pay for everyone else's sins?*

And you can't pastor very long, especially in a big church, without having to answer many questions about evil and suffering:

> *How can a good God allow so much evil and suffering (to six million Jews, for instance)? How can He allow it to happen to innocent children?*
> *Why are some healed while others aren't?*
> *Why aren't the miracles that occurred among God's people in Bible times happening more often today? Is it because we don't have enough faith? Are we too sinful? Must more people pray?*

Harrison Ford once gave the background of a famous scene in an Indiana Jones movie. Originally, he and another character were supposed to go at each other with whips in a lengthy fight. But Ford had the flu and just couldn't face a whole day filming. When the scene was set up and the action began, for a joke, he whipped out a pistol and "shot" his "enemy" dead. The director liked the effect so much he yelled, "Cut!" and told Ford to go back to bed!

God has a "gun"—He has the power to destroy Satan and all evil in an instant. Why hasn't He used it? Why has He put the universe through the agony of a fight that's lasted thousands of years?

And then there are the hard questions about the last days (eschatology):

Why do we have to go through a time of trouble and persecution?

Do we have to go through a period "without a Mediator," without Christ, without the Holy Spirit?

Is there really a judgment going on right now during which our names could come up at any time and—if we're not perfect—be blotted out of the Book of Life?

Who sends the seven last plagues?

Is a good and loving God really going to destroy all the wicked with fire? Can He really do that to His own "children"?

I knew better than to "preach" all these questions in the churches I pastored. But as a pastor, I've been asked them many times. And in Sabbath School classes, over potluck dinners, and in late-night discussions with my pastor friends, I've wrestled with them. In this book I've taken a crack at some answers. I may not have gotten all the answers right—this book certainly won't be the last word. But maybe we can recover at least *some* of the territory Satan has taken by throwing these questions at us for thousands of years.

I know that putting your picture of God "on the table" and opening your understanding of Him to something new can be a little scary. Dick Winn has pointed out that Mary didn't recognize Jesus after the Resurrection. To recognize the resurrected Jesus, she had to let go of her old picture of the precrucifixion Jesus. It can be terrifying to let an old picture of God die, because we wonder what will replace it. But the Resurrection is a promise that God is forever offering us new pictures of Himself—bigger, better, clearer, more accurate, and more triumphant than what we had been sure was "true."

This bigger, better picture of God starts with questions that acknowledge a gap in the evidence, a conflict, an inconsistency. The questions force us to re-examine the evidence and maybe relinquish a cherished idea, letting it die and be buried, all the while trusting that God will soon give us new answers that take in more of the evidence, resolve inconsistencies, and unlock mysteries, until some-day we will see the pure, crystal-clear picture of God as He really is!

WHY WRESTLE WITH THE HARD QUESTIONS?

Does it really matter? Isn't it hopeless to think we'll ever under-stand God anyway? After all, God said, " 'My thoughts are com-pletely different from yours. . . . For just as the heavens are higher than the earth, so are my ways higher than your ways and my thoughts higher than your thoughts' " (Isaiah 55:8, 9, NLT).*

True, we will never master God. True, we will study these myster-ies throughout eternity. God is infinite. He is the "wholly other." But for all kinds of reasons, He still calls us to search.

1. God tells us to study. He says we're to reason together (Isaiah 1:18). He wants us to love Him "with all our minds" (Matthew 22:37). Edward Heppenstall used to say, "Of course it is dangerous to think—but it is more dangerous *not* to think!"[1] God made us to think, to ask questions, to search. And He wants to be known: " 'You will seek me and find me when you seek me with all your heart. I will be found by you' " (Jeremiah 29:13, 14).

2. When we believe wrong ideas about God, it breaks His heart. This debate that we call the great controversy is all about the ques-tions Satan has insinuated about God. It was these questions that started the war in heaven. And it is because God is waiting for the answers to become clear to the entire universe that Christ has de-layed His coming. He can't bear to return until every person has had an adequate opportunity to know the real truth about Him before making an eternal, irreversible decision.

Most of us have grown up visualizing God as ensconced behind the thick walls of His heavenly fortress while we're banging our fists

---

*See also Job 11:7, 8.

on the door trying to persuade Him that we're good enough for Him to let us in. But Revelation 3:20 pictures us inside and God outside, knocking on the door, trying to persuade *us* that He is good enough for us to let Him in. God is the one on trial, not us. We are deciding whether He's the kind of God we want to spend forever with. And so God cares *a lot* about the questions and lies Satan has been putting out there for thousands of years.

Jesus called Satan "the father of lies" (John 8:44). He is the god of this world, blinding people to the truth of the gospel (2 Corinthians 4:3, 4). God is obsessed with showing us the truth. He was totally frustrated with Job's three friends, who, He said, had " 'not spoken of me what is right, as my servant Job has' " (Job 42:8). He wants us to boast only in this—that we "understand and know" Him, that He is "the LORD, who exercises kindness, justice and righteousness on earth" (Jeremiah 9:23, 24).

And isn't it obvious from Revelation 14? There God has a final witness to the world—the 144,000, and they have God's name written on their foreheads. His name stands for His character. God wants the truth about Him to be the final message to go around the world.[2] The 144,000 will have "no lie . . . in their mouths" (verse 5). God cares about the truth. He wants us to know the truth.

3. God sent Christ for the very purpose of answering our questions. Hebrews 1:1-3 says that God tried to use prophets in the past, "but in these last days He has spoken to us by his Son . . . the radiance of God's glory and the exact representation of his being." If the message of the prophets had been totally clear and adequate, Christ's coming wouldn't have been necessary. But Christ *did* come. It *was* necessary. He cares about truth. He wants the questions answered.

And it had to be Christ who came, because only Christ is *exactly* like God. He is God. There is nothing about God that is not exactly like Christ, that is more than Christ, that is different from Christ. "I and the Father are one" (John 10:30). "Anyone who has seen Me has seen the Father" (John 14:9). "No one has ever seen God, but God the One and Only, who is at the Father's side, has made Him known" (John 1:18).

Jesus said over and over again that He is the Truth: "I am the way, the truth, and the life. No one comes to the Father except through me" (John 14:6). Obviously, God cares a lot about what people think of Him; He made the agonizing choice to send the very best to answer the questions once and for all.

4. *What you believe can affect your salvation.* Hebrews 11:6 clearly says that it is not enough to simply believe that God exists; we are to believe that God is One who "rewards those who earnestly seek him." It matters *what* we believe about God. If we are saved by grace "through faith" (Ephesians 2:8), it is obvious that to be saved we have to have faith in the idea of grace—which is another way of saying that we have to believe that God is "grace." Anyone who believes something else about God will not be "saved by grace through faith."

In John 10, Jesus says that there are true shepherds and false shepherds. "My sheep know me," and "they too will listen to my voice." Jesus' voice is the voice of the Good Shepherd, the shepherd of Psalm 23. If that isn't the voice people have learned to recognize, they will follow the wrong shepherd and be lost. So, knowing the truth about God can affect your salvation.

Paul makes it clear that false shepherds and the antichrist will arise *within the church* to distort the truth (2 Thessalonians 2; see also Revelation 13–17). They will teach a caricature of God. People will be lost because they didn't love the truth! Truth matters! The church is supposed to be the pillar of truth. We have to audit every single belief we hold to make sure that it is truly the truth.

I've become a scuba diver recently. My first open-water dive was in Lake Perris in southern California. The visibility was terrible—maybe ten feet. The second dive was off Laguna, on the coast, where we could see maybe fifteen feet. The third was at Catalina, twenty miles off the coast, where we could see probably thirty feet. There we enjoyed the incredible sight of the sunlight filtering through the towering kelp beds. But then I got the opportunity to dive Key Largo in Florida. When I dropped off the back of the boat, I was instantly in a fairy-tale world. Crystal-clear water. Fifty to one hundred feet of visibility. Fish. Coral. Unbelievable. After the dive I said, "This is why I took that class!"

We should have that same experience regarding the character of God. We keep searching, reading, wrestling, fighting through ideas that seem to be inconsistent or mutually exclusive until we finally get to Key Largo: the truth of Christ Himself—crystal-clear, the clearest picture of God this world has ever seen!

5. Questions can get in the way of our truly loving God. As I said earlier, many of us have believed in God, maybe even worked for God. But we've come to a point where we could go no further in truly loving and relating to God without resolving some of our questions about Him. I meet people all the time who are just plain stuck, unable to get past their questions about how God could allow their spouse to die. I had an atheist tell me that he got bogged down on the second commandment: How could God punish his descendents to the third and fourth generations for his sin? It isn't fair. So, we have to wrestle with the hard questions.

6. Questions can get in the way of winning people to God. Bill Hybels says he used to go windsurfing on Lake Michigan with a seeker. For nine years Bill and this man sailed and then "wound down" in a coffee shop, where Bill talked about Christ. Finally, with deep disappointment, Bill asked his friend why he had never accepted Christ. He said, "Because I've always been afraid I would lose more than I would gain."

It's true! Why should anyone "convert" unless they're convinced that the new belief has better answers, more truth, and adds meaning and richness to their lives that weren't there before? If we really dream of taking the gospel to the whole world "and then the end will come," we'd better find a way to make sure the gospel is truly "good news"—better news than whatever they believed before. Jesus said, "I, when I am lifted up from the earth, will draw all men to myself" (John 12:32).

7. *The character of God is the last message to go around the world before Christ can come.* Here's the *coup de grâce:* "The last rays of merciful light, the last message of mercy to be given to the world, is a revelation of His [God's] character of love. The children of God are to manifest His glory. In their own life and character they are to reveal what the grace of God has done for them."[3]

I once believed, without ever thinking about it, that earth's probation would close whenever God decided that time was up. But then I figured out that God is never arbitrary. God won't close the door as long as there is the slightest chance that anyone could still be persuaded to come over to His side. He will ask one final time, "Is there anything else I can do, anything else I can show you?" Only when every single individual on earth has made a personal, voluntary, free, irrevocable choice one way or the other will God close probation.

If that is true, then, if we want the suffering in this world to end, we have to tell the world the truth about God. We have to answer enough of the questions about God so that people can be drawn to Him, fall in love with Him, and see Him for Who He really is—the most incredible Being anyone could possibly imagine. You can't dream up a God better than He already is!

And those of us who love the Sabbath as a day to worship and honor God can't forget the preceding commandment: Don't take the name of God in vain. That means so much more than just avoiding four-letter words. It means knowing and believing the truth about God. In fact, we can't really keep the fourth commandment until we keep the third. We have to tell the world the truth about Him if we hope to have them enjoy twenty-four hours with Him on the Sabbath!

Now, a classic story I've told around the world: Four men are in an airplane. The pilot comes back and tells the passengers, "We're going down; we have only three parachutes, and one of them is mine!" Then he takes one and jumps. The next man proclaims, "I'm the smartest man in the world, and I'm working on the cure for cancer." And he takes a parachute and jumps.

The third man is an old preacher. He says to the fourth passenger, a Boy Scout, "Young man, I've already lived a long life, and I know God. You take that last parachute and jump."

And the Boy Scout says, "Cool it, preacher. The smartest man in the world just jumped with my backpack!"

Obviously, it matters what you jump with! Regarding some important things, being right matters.

Truth matters to God. And it should matter to us.

1. Quoted by Fritz Guy, *Thinking Theologically: Adventist Christianity and the Interpretation of Faith* (Berrien Springs, Mich.: Andrews University Press, 1999), 57.

2. Ellen G. White, *Christ's Object Lessons* (Hagerstown, Md.: Review and Herald), 415.

3. Ibid., 415, 416.

CHAPTER TWO

Nonnegotiable Anchor Points

Years ago, I read a story in a sports magazine about Magic Johnson, the incomparable former basketball player for the Los Angeles Lakers who's a five-time world champion. Magic had grown up in a Christian home in Lansing, Michigan, and had left a fiancée back there while he lived a bohemian, bachelor lifestyle as a rich NBA superstar. A reporter who knew about his Christian upbringing asked him how he could justify his lifestyle. Magic's answer was, essentially, "I'm rich and I'm young. I've got to have fun as long as it lasts. Then I'll get back to my fiancée and to God. God's going to have to wait!" Unfortunately, Magic got HIV before he got back to God.

Like a lot of other people, Magic apparently believed that God is Someone who gets in the way of having a good time. That if God's around, the party's over. That He says, "If it's fun, you can't do it. If it tastes good, you can't eat it. If it looks good, you can't wear it." Where do people get that picture of God?

Before we get into the questions, then, let's nail down certain nonnegotiable anchor points about God.

1. God is not a thief! An old Navajo man and his nephew were walking by a field where some astronauts were training. The old man asked his nephew what they were doing. "They're training to go to the moon!" the nephew replied. The old man got very excited and asked if he could send a message to the moon. He recorded a little message in Navajo and gave the tape to the astronauts.

They had no idea what the old man had said. Everyone for whom they played the tape laughed but refused to translate it. Finally they found a translator. The old man's message: "Look out for these guys; they're out to steal your land!"

That's been Satan's message for thousands of years: "Look out for God—He's out to steal your life!"

If I could choose only one verse to summarize everything I believe about God, I just might pick what Jesus told the Jews: "The thief comes only to steal and kill and destroy; I have come that they may have life, and have it to the full" (John 10:10). The very fact that Jesus felt compelled to say this tells us something incredible—that Satan has somehow so distorted the picture of God that people saw Him as a thief! So the God of the universe has to come down from heaven to set everything straight: "Thieves come to steal and destroy. I am not a thief!"

This verse highlights the central issue of the great controversy between Christ and Satan: Who brings more life, God or the other side? God says, "If you eat of the tree you will surely die." A snake in the tree says, "No, you will not surely die." Who's telling the truth? Satan's constant purpose has been to distort the truth about God, to make God look like a thief. "Don't get too close to God—He'll cheat you out of life!"

"No," Jesus says, "I came to give you life."

But if we're honest, most of us will have to admit that we've unconsciously accepted some version of Satan's lies about God:

• *Evil and suffering:* Either evil comes from God or God chose to allow some suffering to come upon us. Insurance companies call disasters "acts of God." Magic Johnson once said, "God knew what He was doing when He allowed me to get HIV!" (Magic thought he was a good "candidate" because he had such a positive attitude.) At a funeral for six kids who were killed in a highway accident while returning to college from their homes, a preacher said to the other students: "God allowed this to wake some of you up, to get you back to church." No, God came to give life, not to take it away.

• *Prayer:* We somehow have assumed that to persuade God to change His mind and do a miracle, we need to accumulate as many prayers as possible or to get the most important pastors we can find to pray for us. We tell God all kinds of reasons as to why He should reverse course and intervene. I absolutely believe in prayer, but we need to be very careful that our prayer theology doesn't somehow imply that God is reluctant. No, God is not like that. He came to give life, more abundant life!

• *Sabbath:* Instead of showing that the Sabbath is an incredible gift, we've sometimes emphasized rules on how to keep it—and in doing so, made young people feel that God is a thief, taking away life! The Sabbath was a gift for thousands of years before it became a commandment! "The Sabbath was made for man" (Mark 2:27).

• *Stewardship:* People sometimes feel that God and the church are always after money. But those who have really learned the joy of giving strategically to make a difference for God around the world have learned that the ability to give is itself an incredible gift. We get to partner with God all over the world! I've played almost every sport, and I've traveled the world. But I've learned that there is no pleasure like joining with God and a group of people to build an orphanage or a school or a church. There's nothing like making a long-term impact, leaving a legacy. Giving is a gift.

• *Standards:* Whenever we view church standards as negative, restrictive—"You can't go to movies, you can't dance, you can't listen to rock music, you can't sleep together before you get married"—we've bought into Satan's lies. We haven't always been very good at showing kids how these standards give life. Jesus says, "My words are life!" (see John 6:63).

Some software programs can enable computers to *morph* images, blending the characteristics of one person into a picture of someone else. Satan has always done his best to mix his own characteristics into our picture of God.[1] Consequently, millions of people think they are worshiping God when they're actually, unconsciously, worshiping a subtle caricature of God. People see God—who came to give life—as taking life away. And they see Satan—who destroys life—as somehow giving life. All kinds of media perpetuate the lie, and it's all a sacrilege against God! Jesus had to come down to say, "I am the way and the truth and the life" (John 14:6).

Satan's ultimate lie is that if you get serious about God, you'll lose out on the good times of life. But Jesus says, "I am not a thief. I came to give life!"

2. We need not fear God. Over the past few years another scripture has become a defining passage for me: "The angel said to them, 'Do not be afraid. I bring you good news of great joy' " (Luke 2:10). In the book *Steps to Christ,* Ellen G. White wrote that Satan has done everything he can to get people to look at God with fear.[2] For thousands of years all the millions of heavenly angels had watched silently as Satan spread this false picture of God all over the world. So when the angels finally got the chance to speak, what were their first words? "Do not be afraid."

God doesn't want anyone to worship Him out of fear. That's why He came as a baby. The angels said to the shepherds, "Go to Him.

Don't be afraid. He's a baby. No one has to be afraid of a baby." And He never changes: "Jesus Christ is the same yesterday and today and forever" (Hebrews 13:8).

After Joseph Stalin died, Nikita Khrushchev, the new leader of the Soviet Union, was discussing the atrocities Stalin had committed against the Russian people. Someone in the crowd shouted out, "You were there. Why didn't you stop him?"

Khrushchev whirled around and roared, "Who said that?" There was total silence in the room. Then, in a quiet voice, he said, "Now you know why." Power and punishment and Gulag camps in Siberia are effective. Machiavelli wrote, "It would be nice to mix fear and love. But since fear and love can hardly exist together, if we must choose between them, it is far safer to be feared than loved."

However, the angels said, "Do not be afraid!" "It is Satan's constant effort to misrepresent the character of God. . . . At the same time he causes them to cherish false conceptions of God so that they regard Him with fear . . . rather than love."[3] John wrote, "Perfect love drives out fear" (1 John 4:18). And Jesus came down "to enable us to serve him without fear" (Luke 1:74).* So we need to go through all our beliefs and make sure we have nothing of fear anywhere.

3. God is good news! The angel said, "Do not be afraid. I bring you good news of great joy!" (Luke 2:10). Everything about God has to be good news—the angel said so! God is only good news, nothing but good news. We can't accept a pass/fail system, where, as long as there is more good news than bad news, we give God a C+ and let Him pass. He has to get an A in every subject. He has to be good news from alpha to omega.

When we figure out that He is only good news, it won't take long for us to carry the gospel to the entire world. My family went to a

---

*See also Romans 8:15 and Ellen G. White, *The Desire of Ages* (Nampa, Idaho: Pacific Press, 1940), 480.

wedding in Pasadena during the seventh game of the NBA playoffs between the Los Angeles Lakers and the Portland Trailblazers. The reception was at the Pasadena city hall, so while we were driving there, my two sons were listening to Chick Hearn's broadcast of the game. It was the fourth quarter, and the Lakers were down by fifteen. But the Trailblazers began to miss, and Kobe and Shaq began to score.

We got to the parking lot, and Hilda, my wife, said, "Dan, we've got to go—we're going to be late." But two little boys in the back seat begged, "Mom, we can't go in now. They're catching up!" I looked around the parking lot. No one else was leaving their cars either!

When there were just two minutes left in the game and the Lakers had almost caught up, Hilda said, "Dan, we've *got* to go." So I turned the radio off, and we went into the reception. Within five minutes, people started to whisper, "Did you hear? The Lakers won!" In minutes, everyone had the news. That's what's going to happen some day, when we truly believe that God is nothing but good news!

4. God brings great joy! Next, the angel said, "I bring you good news of *great joy!*" (Luke 2:10). I saw a bit of an Elton John concert on TV. (Somehow I missed Elton John when I was growing up.) On this broadcast, I saw thirty thousand people who stood for three hours in Madison Square Garden, waving, clapping, and singing along. They knew all the words to the songs. I wondered, *When are people going to do this for God—be willing to stand for hours, clapping, knowing all the words, full of great joy?* Someday it's going to happen!

5. "He ain't heavy!" For far too many people, God and religion feel heavy on the soul. These people are exhausted; they're carrying a load of guilt or of legalism—never feeling good enough for God, worried about the judgment, terrified of being lost. Jesus said: "Come to me, all you who are weary . . . and I will give you rest. . . . For my yoke is easy and my burden is light" (Matthew 11:28-30).

This is another verse that has become a defining verse for me. It's pretty clear that if our religion ever feels heavy, we didn't get it from God, because Jesus said, "My yoke is easy and my burden is light." So again we have to go through all our beliefs, making sure we have nothing that feels "heavy."

Charles Swindoll tells an old story about a man who was walking through an airport terminal. Another man comes up and asks, "Do you know what time it is?" The first man sets down his two heavy suitcases, checks his watch, and tells him not only the local time, but also the time in Singapore, the weather in London, and the Lakers' score.

"That watch can tell you all that? I'll give you five hundred dollars for that watch right now!"

"No, it's not for sale."

"A thousand dollars."

"No, it's an heirloom. I'm giving it to my son. There's no other one like it in the world."

"Five thousand dollars cash. Right now."

"OK."

The purchaser hands over the money, takes the watch, and turns to leave. Then the seller points to the two suitcases and says, "Don't forget the batteries!"[4]

Many people love Christianity at first—Jesus, love, forgiveness, heaven. Then someone gives them a long list of rules, or they get a taste of church politics, and suddenly, religion feels heavy. It's seems not to be worth it. But Jesus says, "My yoke is easy and my burden is light."

He ain't heavy!

6. God is righteous. One of my favorite verses is: "The LORD our God is righteous in everything he does" (Daniel 9:14). God does everything right. Sometimes we're tempted to think that if we were

God, we would have done things differently—we would have destroyed Satan or we would have intervened in this situation or we would have answered that prayer instantly. "You blew that one, God." But think about what we're saying about God. And remember, God is righteous! When we see the end from the beginning, we will all say in unison, "The LORD our God is righteous in everything he does." We would have done it *exactly* as He did it. At the conclusion of the great controversy, every intelligent being who has ever lived will bow down before the maligned God of the universe and acknowledge that He has been absolutely righteous (see Revelation 15:3, 4; 19:2; Philippians 2:9-11).

A corollary is that God is an awesome God. He is perfect, infinitely perfect. God is far beyond the very best god we could dream up. "No eye has seen, no ear has heard, no mind has conceived what God has prepared for those who love Him" (1 Corinthians 2:9). This verse refers to salvation and heaven—but of course, those are all about God!

7. God makes sense. One of Satan's central accusations has been that God is arbitrary. As a young preacher, I used to say that God wants us to obey even when what He asks makes no sense to us. No! God always wants what He asks to make sense. He wants us to love Him with all our *mind* (Matthew 22:37). He's the one who invites us, "Come now, let us reason together" (Isaiah 1:18). He wants us never to be embarrassed, never to be ashamed (Romans 1:16). Everything we say about God or about our church or our religion has to be something we are proud to share because it is so logical (even if we can't solve everything yet!).

8. God is our friend. Jesus said, "I no longer call you servants, because a servant does not know his master's business. Instead, I have called you friends" (John 15:15). The night before He would die,

Jesus gave His greatest description of the kind of relationship He longs to have with us: "I have called you friends." Everything we say about God has to be consistent with that. We're friends. We're not in a master/servant relationship. We're friends.

9. God the Father and God the Son are exactly alike. Another nonnegotiable anchor point is that God the Father is exactly like the Son. This belief lies at the heart of Christianity. Michael Ramsey wrote somewhere: "In the Father there is no un-Christlikeness." You cannot split them up. One is not nicer than the other. One doesn't love us more than the other. Jesus said, "Anyone who has seen me has seen the Father" (John 14:9).

10. God is love. Of course, the final, ultimate nonnegotiable anchor point about God is love. Everything we say about God has to be consistent with "God is love." Love is the default. Love is the controlling metaphor.[5]

God's love is perfect. He loves His enemies (Matthew 5:43-48). His love never stops. You can't love any more than God. You can't imagine a God who can love more than God loves. There is nothing you can do to make God love you more. And nothing you could ever do—no sin you could ever commit—could ever cause God to love you any less.

When you get to heaven and you see God face to face for the first time, you'll feel like you've known Him before. You'll recognize the best of all your favorite people in Him. All the best people in your life were a gift from God, to give you a taste of what He's really like. All the best moments of love and friendship down here were delights straight from His heart to yours; He was hoping that you would recognize Him in them, that they would draw you to Him, the ultimate source of all love.[6]

We must resolve all the questions we'll wrestle with in this book—the hard questions from the Old Testament, the tough questions about why God allows evil and suffering, why He doesn't step in more, why Jesus had to die, and how the wicked die at the end of the world—in favor of God's love. There can be no exceptions, no compromises, no time outs, no moral leftovers! God is love—period! "Whoever does not love does not know God, because God is love" (1 John 4:8).

So, there's the list of nonnegotiable anchor points about God. We start with them!

1. See Ellen G. White, *Signs of the Times,* January 20, 1890.

2. See Ellen G. White, *Steps to Christ,* (Nampa, Idaho: Pacific Press, 1990) 10, 11.

3. Ellen G. White, *The Great Controversy* (Nampa, Idaho: Pacific Press, 1950), 569.

4. Charles R. Swindoll, *Simple Faith* (Minneapolis: Grason, 1991), xviii-xix.

5. Richard Rice, Clark Pinnock, John Sanders, William Hasker, and David Basinger, *The Openness of God* (Downers Grove, Ill.: InterVarsity Press, 1994), 15-21. The "controlling metaphor" phrase is attributed to Terence Fretheim, *The Suffering of God: An Old Testament Perspective* (Philadelphia: Fortress, 1984), 11.

6. C. S. Lewis, *The Four Loves* (San Diego: Harcourt Brace Jovanovich, 1960), 191.

CHAPTER THREE

The Tree, the Cross, and the Fire

I heard a great story on a sermon tape by Rico Tice, of All Souls Church in London. He had spent his day off in the living room of his parents' home, teaching his young nephews, two and five years old, how to play rugby. The little boys got so excited about the game that one of them grabbed a flowerpot and dumped the dirt all over grandma's plush white carpet so that it would be more like a real rugby field. Then Grandma walked into the room and saw the dirt all over the floor. Instantly, she scooped up the culprit, hugged him, and said, "Let's go have lunch!"

Is God like that? Or is He like the soccer coach I saw one Sunday afternoon? His twelve-year-old daughter, a bit chubby, was the goalie. When a girl on the other side had a breakaway and scored against her, he went crazy! He walked out on the field and screamed at his daughter—in front of all her friends and their parents—for being so slow and fat. How is she going to feel when a preacher says, "God is like a father"?

We're approaching a continental divide, a major fork in the road. How we interpret one passage in the Bible will determine our picture of God, all our theology about Him. That passage reports what God said in the garden of Eden: "The LORD God commanded the man, 'You are free to eat from any tree in the garden; but you must not eat from the tree of the knowledge of good and evil, for when you eat of it you will surely die' " (Genesis 2:16, 17).

THE TREE

Ultimately, virtually everything we say about God, the Cross, the atonement, and last things starts with what we believe about God's intent in these two verses. The traditional model most of us learned when we were young sees God as threatening divine punishment as the consequence of violating His command. God is holy, and sin is terribly offensive to Him. He could show how serious sin is and how much He hates it only by making eternal death its penalty.

Those who criticize this view suggest that no loving parent would make eternal death the penalty for a single sin, a single instance of rebellion, so how can we believe that a loving God would destroy His own children for one sin? It's as though God were saying, "Love Me or I'll kill you." Those who believe in this model usually admit no parent would do this, but they still maintain that this is the picture we have in the Bible—a just, righteous God who sees death as the only effective punishment for sin.

There's an alternate model. It says that God wasn't threatening punishment here. He was instead giving a *loving warning of the natural consequences* of choosing to live autonomously from Him. He's not the kind of God who could destroy His own children for their first sin and do the actual killing Himself. Those who hold to this model see God as the only Source of life in the universe, and they believe that in Eden He was giving a warning of the natural laws of cause and effect: If you choose to disconnect yourself from the only Source of life, you will die, as surely as a vacuum cleaner stops the moment its cord is pulled from the outlet. God was underlining a law of the universe: Life comes from God alone. If someone releases the hand brake of a car parked at the top of a hill, the car will start rolling and pick up speed until finally it careens out of control. That, in this model, is what happened at the Tree. God let go of the hand brake—He respects free choice—and natural consequences followed.

Mark Ford wrote a parable[1] years ago that went something like this: A rich young man had fallen in love with a beautiful young woman. On the day he was planning to propose to her, he took her out to the mountains. There, nestled in the forest, was a magnificent mansion. He said, "If we get married, this is where we will live." She was ready to say "Yes!" right then, but he said, "Wait." He gave her a tour of every room, and she could picture herself the queen of the mansion, but he said, "Not yet." He then took her out behind the mansion, where she was horrified to see a fresh grave and tombstone.

"What is this?" she asked.

"I buried my first wife, Mary, here. We were so much in love— we were magic, so romantic. I thought we would last forever. But I began to sense I was losing her. I did everything I could to hold on to her. But finally, at my wits' end, I did what I had to do—I killed her." Then the young man knelt down on one knee before her and said, "Now, will you marry me? Will you love me forever?"

Of course, the story is just a parable. But it was Ford's picture of what our first model above is really saying about God. Can we really imagine God saying to Adam and Eve, "I want you to love Me forever. But if you don't, you'll have to die; I'll have to kill you"? At first glance that model seems contrary to all the nonnegotiable anchor points of the last chapter. And the Bible contains a number of verses that seem to support the "natural consequences" model instead: "A man reaps what he sows" (Galatians 6:7). "A man's own folly ruins his life, yet his heart rages against the LORD" (Proverbs 19:3). "The wages of sin is death" (Romans 6:23). "Perfect love drives out fear, because fear has to do with punishment" (1 John 4:18).

Of the death of the wicked, Ellen White wrote:

> This is not an act of arbitrary power on the part of God. The rejecters of His mercy reap that which they have sown. God is the fountain of life; and when one chooses the service of sin, he separates from God, and thus cuts himself off from life. . . . God gives them existence for a time that they may develop their character and reveal their principles. This accomplished, they receive the results of their own choice.[2]

In the Bible, the law of sin and death is all about natural consequences. Smoking leads to cancer. Sin hurts us. Sin cheats us of life. Have you heard of the Darwin Awards? They're given, posthumously, to those who have advanced the gene pool the most by dying as the result of stupid choices they made. That's what God was saying at the Tree—sin has consequences.

Jesus' parable of the prodigal son illustrates this point clearly. The prodigal son went to a far country and lived the high life until all his money was gone and he ended up in a pigsty. The father didn't punish him by sending him to the pigsty. The son went there as the natural consequence of choosing to live apart from the father and squandering the "life" that the father had graciously given him.

A friend of mine, David Mayor, an emergency room doctor in Hinsdale, Illinois, told me about an old lady who came into the emergency room coughing and wheezing. He got her onto a bed, saw how blue she was, and started to give her oxygen. The oxygen began turning her skin pink again. Mayor told her he needed to admit her immediately to save her life. But she said no, this was normal. She said she just wanted help with the pus oozing from her eyes, and then she asked for a cigarette.

Mayor told her she would have to quit smoking or she would die. He told her they needed to admit her right away. But she refused and kept asking for a cigarette. Finally, he was forced to get her to sign a release form, admitting that she was leaving the emergency room of her own choice, against the best advice of the doctors. She walked out of the emergency room turning blue again, wheezing and coughing and still asking for a cigarette while Mayor stood at the door, saying, "Please don't go, you'll die out there." That's the picture we have of God at the Tree, giving a loving warning of the terrible natural consequences of trying to live on our own in this world.

THE CROSS

So, there's a fork in the road at the Tree, and the branch we take has huge implications for what we believe happened at the Cross— for what we believe about the atonement Christ provided. He came to bear the consequences of sin. If those consequences were divine punishment, then Christ bore our divine punishment on the Cross as our substitute. But if those consequences were natural, then in some way the Godhead endured the natural consequences of sin in our place at the Cross.

The traditional model: This model says God dictated at the Tree that eternal death was the just penalty for sin. However, because God was "not willing that any should perish," He sent His Son to take the divine punishment in our place, as our substitute. By logical extension, that implies that the punishment Christ endured on the Cross came from His own Father. To say it plainly, God killed Christ in our place. For two thousand years this has been the majority view, though not usually stated quite so directly. God poured out His divine wrath on Christ at the Cross.

However, during the centuries of theological debate, many have found this model troubling. Here are some of the reasons:

1. It seems to contradict the character of God. How could a God of love kill His own Son? No sane earthly parent could do that—and God's love is far beyond that of any parent.

2. It doesn't fit the Trinity—that God is One. We believe that God has chosen to express His reality and identity through the Trinity, through the three "faces" or "persons" of God. But Christians are adamant that we are monotheistic: "Hear, O Israel: The LORD our God, the LORD is one" (Deuteronomy 6:4; see also John 10:30). We have to be very careful that our theology of the Cross doesn't split and divide the Trinity, having one Person crucify one of the others. And, as we noted in the previous chapter, one of our nonnegotiable anchor points is our belief that God the Father and God the Son are exactly alike in character.

3. This model seems to drive a wedge into the unity of God. The traditional view says that His justice demands that the penalty of death be upheld while His great love demands that He forgive, putting God into great conflict. It says that the conflict is resolved in Christ. He both satisfied God's justice and demonstrated His love on the Cross.

But some argue that the unity of God can't allow that sort of deep-seated conflict. God isn't conflicted, torn, dysfunctional, or in tension with Himself. Yes, He's complex and multifaceted, but He is also absolutely unified, indissolubly One. He isn't split into two halves, each leading to an opposite conclusion.

It's also been suggested that we need to be careful about this tension between God's love and His justice. God's forgiveness isn't something that has to overcome, conquer, or trump His justice. In the Psalms, justice is positive. David continually begs God to manifest His justice, because he knows that God's justice will be in his favor. God's justice will reveal itself in love, forgiveness, grace, and awesome power. Also, we're told, "If we confess our sins, he is faithful and just and will forgive us our sins" (1 John 1:9). God's justice isn't contrary to His forgiveness. He forgives *because* He is just! His justice and His faithful love lead to the same conclusion, rather than to opposite conclusions.

The Tree, the Cross, and the Fire

4. Making forgiveness dependent on the Cross reverses the true order. Jesus tells *us* to forgive "seventy times seven" times, to turn the other cheek, and to love our enemies—why doesn't He do the same? If we don't need someone to "sacrifice" to us to persuade us to forgive, why does God? Jesus, on the Cross, *before* He had actually died, freely offered His and His Father's forgiveness to those crucifying Him: "Father, forgive them; for they know not what they do" (Luke 23:34, KJV). Ellen G. White wrote that His prayer for forgiveness "took in every sinner that had lived or should live, from the beginning of the world to the end of time."[3]

Clearly, it was not the Cross that turned God into a forgiver.

> This great sacrifice was not made in order to create in the Father's heart a love for man, not to make Him willing to save. No, no! "God so loved the world, that He gave His only-begotten Son." John 3:16. The Father loves us, not because of the great propitiation, but He provided the propitiation because He loves us.[4]

It is absolutely critical that Christianity be able to distinguish clearly what we believe happened on the Cross from the sacrifices that are part of paganism, in which people have to offer sacrifices to appease the fierce anger of the gods.

5. Finally, the traditional position seems to contradict some of the statements within Scripture that clearly say that the Father didn't kill Christ. Jesus Himself said, "I lay down my life—only to take it up again. No one takes it from me, but I lay it down of my own accord" (John 10:17, 18). And on the Cross itself, He cried out: "My God, My God, why have you forsaken me?" (Matthew 27:46). He *didn't* say, "Why are You killing Me?"

So those who have been troubled by the traditional model believe that God doesn't kill sinners, at least in the sense of the second death. If God kills sinners, then God should have killed Christ. Christ had taken on all the sins that have been committed or will ever be committed (1 John 2:2). But if God didn't kill Christ, can we then conclude that God and Christ *together* endured the natural consequences of sin?

The challenge has been to explore the Cross and the atonement, to discover if there is a way to preserve the necessity of the Cross, the uniqueness of the sacrifice, and the concept of substitution, without unwittingly doing damage to the character of God in the process. Is it possible to be absolutely true to the centrality of the Cross within Christianity, without allowing any traces of paganism into our understanding of the Cross?*

The natural-consequences model: An alternative model has been developed that takes another branch of the fork at the Tree. It starts with the assumption that God was giving a loving warning of the natural consequences of choosing to live apart from Him, the Source of life in the universe. Satan then introduced his central challenge: " 'Did God really say, "You must not eat from any tree in the garden?" . . . You will not surely die' " (Genesis 3:1-4). The entire great controversy concerns that fundamental issue and who was telling the truth. Can people live apart from God, as Satan claimed he was demonstrating? Or will those who try, die, as God warned?

Well, Adam and Eve ate from the Tree. They sinned. Then God had to make a terrible choice: *How would He teach them once and for all the fundamental reality of the universe?* He could let Adam die, and Eve would quickly learn. Or He could let Eve die, and Adam would quickly get it. But either way God would lose half the class, and He is "not wanting anyone to perish" (2 Peter 3:9). So He sent a substitute to demonstrate to the entire watching universe the answers to

---

*At the same time we have to humbly acknowledge that if it is true that we will continue to study the mystery of the atonement throughout eternity, it is extreme hubris to assume that we will master it all here and now! See White, *Great Controversy,* 651.

the fundamental questions: (1) Can we live apart from God? (2) How does God feel about sinners? (3) How does God treat sinners? (4) Who is telling the truth?

Christ came down to this earth to die for sinners, yes. To "seek and save the lost," yes. But the ultimate existence of His universe and kingdom was on the line, depending on whether He could convince everyone watching that He is telling the truth and that He is the kind of God we would feel safe with and want to be with forever.

So the journey began. "The Lamb that was slain from the creation of the world" (Revelation 13:8) was going to come here to die. Christ and the Father had to say Goodbye. Imagine what that goodbye must have been like. After trillions of years of being absolutely One, their "community" was going to be ripped apart. When I was a child, every time our family got on a plane to return to the mission field in Thailand, we had to endure a goodbye at our grandfather Venden's house. The last prayer was his; he would pour out his heart to God, pleading for our safety. Then we would all hug and cry, knowing that it would be years before we would see each other again. But we were parting for only a few years—the Father and the Son were risking never being together again! And Jesus came down as a baby. He had no memory of His role and place in heaven. He was completely human, having given up the use of the attributes of divinity—even though He was still fully God (Philippians 2:5-8).

We're told that as Jesus went to the Temple and saw the lambs being sacrificed, He began to get the inkling that somehow His life was bound up with these lambs.[5] He knew the story of His birth, and He knew that He was born to die. He spoke about it repeatedly: "I, when I am lifted up from the earth, will draw all men to myself" (John 12:32). "The good shepherd lays down his life for the sheep" (John 10:11).

Then in the garden, His last night before the Cross—the Last Supper over—He separated Himself from His exhausted disciples after asking them to pray. He was beginning to feel the burden of the Cross, the excruciating sense of guilt for all the sins of all the people who have ever lived or will ever live. This is no "paper" guilt. He literally felt the pain and misery of every rape, every murder, every ugly word, every adultery, every lie, every act of violence.

What else did He feel? *Separation.* We're told He clung to the ground to keep from slipping any further from the Father.[6] That's what sin does; it separates us from the Father. Not that God goes anywhere. Nothing separates us from God's love (Romans 8:38, 39). God loves His enemies just the same as His friends. The prodigal's father loved the prodigal as much as he loved the elder brother. But Christ was feeling what sin does to the sinner.

Christ felt the wrath of the Father against sin. What does God do when He feels "wrath" toward sin and sinners? He "gives them up" (Romans 1:18, 24, 26, 28). He gives them over to the natural consequences of their choices. He lets the hand brake go. The sinner "reaps what he sows." So, here's the answer to one of the major questions: What does God do when people choose sin anyway? *He lets them go.* God is absolutely committed to respecting free choice, and so He honors people's free choice to live apart from Him, and He lets them go.

When we say that Christ absorbed the wrath of the Father, what did He experience? He experienced God letting Him go. "My God, my God, why have you forsaken me?" (Matthew 27:46) "He was delivered over to death for our sins" (Romans 4:25). "How can I give you up, Ephraim? How can I hand you over, Israel?" (Hosea 11:8) Jesus died as the Godforsaken God—God Himself, forsaken by God, feeling the loss of the oneness of the Trinity they had experienced and shared together from eternity.

So Christ endured the agony of the second death, experiencing the natural consequences of sin. But His Father was not killing Him. One advantage of this model is that it does not divide the Trinity.

The Tree, the Cross, and the Fire

Christ and the Father are together experiencing the loss and separation that sin causes. The Father feels the loss of the Son as much as the Son feels the loss of the Father. As Jürgen Moltmann has written, "The Fatherlessness of the Son is matched by the Sonlessness of the Father."[7]

The entire universe sees once and for all that God told the truth at the Tree: "If you sin, you will surely die." Satan was wrong. Sin kills. We cannot live apart from God. The Cross proves it, settles it. "You *will* surely die"—but not at the hands of a loving God. He is not like that. No loving parent would do it; God won't do it. But God so loved the world that He was willing to send His Son as a substitute to make clear to the world the fundamental reality—the law of cause and effect. If we leave the Father's house, we *will* end up in a pigsty.

I use parables to try to illustrate what really is beyond illustration. Let's try one here: One day Jesus is walking with some friends on a beautiful beach. Some of them decide to go swimming. Jesus says, "Please don't go swimming in that bay. There are sharks in that bay."

The friends say, "We've never seen any sharks here."

Jesus pleads with them, but some start heading toward the water. Then they see a man swimming in the bay. He says, "Come on in; the water's fine."

"What about sharks?" they ask.

"Is Jesus telling you there are sharks here? There are no sharks here. He just keeps telling people that so they won't have any fun. This is the best beach—no sharks."

Some of the group decide to go in. Before they get very far, Jesus wades into the water and starts swimming—until there's a terrible crunching sound. A shark drags Jesus down, and He drowns.

The group buries Jesus on the beach. On His grave they post a little sign that reads: "Please don't swim here. It's full of sharks. Jesus died so we could live now that we know about the sharks."

Jesus suffered all the violence that sin causes, hoping that we will learn vicariously that sin kills.

THE FIRE

The choice we make at the fork in the road, at the Tree in the garden, leads inevitably to what we will conclude about how the wicked will be removed at the end of the world. *Whatever we decide at the Tree will also be true of the Cross and of the Fire at the end of the world.*

If a person believes that at the Tree, God was threatening divine punishment that He would administer Himself, then it is logical to believe that at the Cross, Christ takes the Father's wrath and punishment upon Himself. And it would be logical to believe that the wicked who have refused to accept the atonement that the Substitute provided for them will endure that same wrath and punishment at the second death.

On the other hand, we may choose to believe that, at the Tree, God was giving a loving warning of the natural consequences of sin. Then we'll most likely understand the Cross in terms of the Father and the Son together experiencing the natural consequences of sin in the terrible separation They endured from Friday to Sunday. And we'll most likely believe that the wicked will endure the natural consequences of sin, the separation from God as the Source of life, at the end of the world, rather than enduring the punishment of eternal death at the hands of God.

We have to be consistent. If, at the Tree, God was outlining one of the fundamental realities of the universe—that those who sin will surely die the second death—and if Christ died the second death in our place, then what we believe about the Tree affects what we believe about the Cross. And if Christ died the second death in our place, then we can look at the Cross to understand the basic reality that will occur at the second death. If we see divine punishment at the Tree, then we'll see divine punishment at the Cross and at the Fire. But if we see natural consequences at the Tree, then we would see natural consequences at the Cross and the Fire. If Christ died at the hands of an angry God, then that is how the wicked who reject Christ will die. But if Christ died instead because God "let Him go" to the natural consequences of the sins He vicariously took upon Himself, then that is how the wicked will die the second death—God will "let them go" to experience the natural consequences of separation from Him.

Good Christians, Christians who are committed to the Bible, have disagreed about these issues for a long time. No doubt people holding either view can be saved. Perhaps someday we'll find another view that will resolve the issue. But our goal is to see God at His very best, to know a God consistent with the nonnegotiable anchor points listed in chapter two. So, with great respect for each other, we keep studying!

1. Mark Ford, "2 Stories About God," *Insight*, August 12, 1989, 2-5.
2. White, *Desire of Ages*, 764.
3. Ibid., 745.
4. White, *Steps to Christ*, 13.
5. White, *Desire of Ages*, 78.
6. Ibid., 685-697.
7. Jürgen Moltmann, *The Crucified God* (Minneapolis: Fortress, 1993), 243.

EXCURSUS A

Certain questions often come up at this point, and you may wish to go directly to the chapters that wrestle with them in greater detail. However, I'll suggest a few brief answers here:

Q: What about substitution? Doesn't this alternative model lean toward the "moral influence theory" and weaken the idea of substitution?

A: I couldn't accept any model that didn't have a clear-cut substitution concept. That motif is just too clear in Scripture to be ignored (see Isaiah 53, etc.). Christ died in our place—period. This model fine-tunes the process of substitution, but clearly has Christ coming to die in our place. (For more detail, see chapter 4.)

Q: If people can be saved by responding to any one of several revelations of God's love, doesn't that reduce the unique necessity of the Cross? Did Christ really have to die?

A. Yes, we believe Christ did have to die. Fundamental questions about the universe had to be answered. People needed to know the truth about the heart of God, how God treats sinners, and what sin does. Our church has traditionally believed that millions will be saved who have never actually heard the name of Christ—but we believe they will be saved *because of* Christ. So, yes, Christ had to die.

Q: Are you saying that God never kills?

A. No. I make a clear distinction between "first death" (sleep) and "second death." While some of the disasters in the Old Testament might be explained by natural events, it is certainly difficult to explain them all away. It appears that God Himself did put people to sleep in the first death (see chapter 7). But I am suggesting that He is not the active agent in the second death; He doesn't actually destroy eternally His own children. Instead, He "lets them go" to experience the natural consequences of sin (see chapter 11).

Q: When Jesus died, He rose again. How is that substitution? The second death is supposed to be eternal.

A. Just as Jonah, down in the belly of the whale, experienced all the emotions of dying, and just as Abraham and Isaac also experienced all the emotions of separation and death on Mount Horeb, so Christ experienced all the emotions of dying the second death as an eternal separation from the love of the Father. He had no absolute assurance that He would ever see His Father again. He could not see "through the portals of the tomb" (see Ellen G. White, *Desire of Ages*, 753).

Q: Doesn't this view reduce the justice of God too much? Won't it remove the motivation for people to quit sinning?

A. God doesn't want anyone to come to Him out of fear (1 John 4:18). He is a Lover who wants only converts drawn and won by His love (Jeremiah 31:3; John 12:32; Song of Solomon). If fear of hell and the justice of God are the only reasons hardened sinners are willing to come to God, then something is wrong. God wants people to be drawn and held by the incredible good news of the gospel.

But if it's fear you want(!)—well, the Cross is a microcosm of the second death at the end of the world. The second death will be as horrible experientially as what Christ endured on the Cross. So this view in no way reduces the agony of the wicked at the end of time—it just puts the blame where it belongs, on the natural consequences of sin rather than on a loving God. No one is going to "get away with it!" No one is going to get off scot-free. The second death is going to be horrible, unendurable. The wicked will certainly experience "justice." But it will come naturally, not at the hands of God.

CHAPTER FOUR

The Godforsaken God

A group of boys used to gather in the parking lot after church and tell stories. They told the same stories over and over again, and they laughed at the same old punch lines. Then someone got the idea that numbering the stories would make it all easier. Someone would say "Number thirty-four!" and they'd all laugh. And someone else would say, "Number sixteen," and they'd all giggle. After a while, however, they couldn't remember which stories went with which numbers or even what the stories were. All they knew was that number thirty-four was really funny!

Could that happen to with us when we talk about the Cross? We can talk Cross-language, we can sing Cross songs, we can put crosses up on our churches and hang them around our neck—but can we still remember the original "old, old story"?

We know we will never fully penetrate the mystery of the Cross. But we're told to meditate an hour a day on the Cross.[1] We're told to lift up the Cross (John 12:32). Paul said, "I resolved to know nothing . . . except Jesus Christ and him crucified," and "May I never boast except in the cross of our Lord Jesus Christ, through which the world has been crucified to me, and I to the world" (1 Corinthians 2:2; Galatians 6:14). Obviously, the Cross is the last word on God, the pinnacle of God's revelation of His character to us through Jesus Christ, the centerpiece of salvation history. And so we keep on trying to search and dig in order to penetrate its deep, central meaning.

MODELS AND METAPHORS

At first the apostles had little or no idea of the cosmic meaning of the Cross. Jesus had told them repeatedly that He would be crucified, yet when it happened they had no idea what was going on. Soon, however, the light began to dawn that somehow this event had salvation implications—that somehow Christ had died "for us" (see 1 Corinthians 15:3-5). The famous song "He's Alive" pictures Peter realizing, "He's alive, and I'm forgiven—Heaven's gates are open wide." The early church figured out that the Cross somehow meant forgiveness and an open door to heaven, to God.

Gradually, the church began to develop a theology of the Cross, and statements about the Cross were woven into the early creeds. But the problem has been that the church never achieved a consensus view of how the crucifixion actually "worked." Why did Jesus have to die? How does one man's death somehow "pay" for everyone else's sins? What does the Cross have to do with forgiveness and mercy and grace?

Theologians have developed certain models to try to interpret the spiritual truths rooted in the Cross. The Bible is not a book of systematic theology; it isn't divided into sections that clearly and concisely spell out various doctrines. We have to pull themes and texts from all over Scripture and try to construct a model that takes every text and theme seriously and makes sense of all of them while answering the deepest questions and needs of human beings.

During two thousand years of reflecting on the meaning of the Cross, people have come up with various models. The challenge is that no one model has achieved total consensus within the church. Each of the models has strengths and strands of truth that everyone agrees on. But all of the models also have implications that many people find troubling.

In writing about the Cross, the biblical authors relied heavily on metaphors: "ransom," "reconciliation," "sacrifice," "justification," "payment," etc. They reached into their world and found the best illustrations they could to illustrate abstract spiritual concepts of salvation. My son Alex had about ten words at his disposal when he first began to speak. When he saw a dog—or a horse or a cow, he would point and say, "Doggie!" When he saw a car—or a truck or a motorcycle, he would say, "Car!" He had to use one of those ten words to name everything he saw. Similarly, the Bible writers were forced to talk about otherworldly spiritual realities within the limitations of their earthly language and ideas. They would meet God and then come back and tell us, "God is a shepherd," "a father," "a king," "a rock," "an eagle," etc.

Here, then, are some basic points we need to know when we're studying the biblical models and metaphors:

1. They all are based on and include truth rooted in Scripture.

2. Each one is a window into truth.

3. Because they are "human" concepts, they are a mixture of concepts of divine truth *and* some concepts that might not be absolutely accurate depictions of God and His character. No illustration "stands on all fours."

4. No one model or metaphor in and of itself portrays the whole truth about God and salvation. We need several or all of the models and metaphors in order to approach the full picture.

5. God has used each of the models and metaphors to draw people to the gospel.

6. Differing people may find spiritual clarity in differing models and metaphors.

7. Each model or metaphor helps correct for the weaknesses of the others.

8. Because these models and metaphors are the products of the human writers as well as of inspiration,[2] they each reflect those writers—their background and spirituality. They were also shaped to fit the people they were written for. Understanding that background can help immeasurably in trying to ferret out the eternal truth that these models and metaphors transmit. But we also have to admit that all models and metaphors have limits, so pressing them too far can distort our picture of God and contradict the rest of the Bible.

For example, the Bible uses the king/kingdom motif throughout. The picture of "God as king" brings all kinds of powerful concepts quickly to mind: richness, power, protection, a kingdom, and mansions. But it can also bring some very negative baggage with it: ruthlessness, injustice, tyranny, distance, and ostentatiousness. Obviously, the Bible writers took a big risk, hoping that we would apply the first set of traits to God, but not the second set. Combining that metaphor with others, such as the Good Shepherd, provides some balance and helps the reader eliminate the negative baggage.

SATISFACTION MODEL/ANSELM OF CANTERBURY

Now let's look at the primary models of the Cross.* Theologians have wrestled with the "transaction" metaphors in the New Testament—the ideas of ransom, payment, redemption, and sacrifice. While these metaphors have their differences, each contains the idea that as sinners, we are in a serious predicament (kidnapped, in debt, in slavery) from which we cannot save ourselves. Someone else must save us by providing some sort of payment.

The problem was always in identifying who would receive the "payment." Clearly, the devil caused our predicament, so the logical answer seemed to be that he was the one demanding the payment.

---

*For this discussion on the atonement, I have depended on authors such as Provonsha and Grensted (see the endnotes) and historical theology sources, such as Alister McGrath, *Christian Theology: An Introduction*, 3rd ed. (Malden, Mass.: Blackwell Publishers, 2001).

God, then, offered Christ as the payment; the devil was satisfied, and we go free. One of the problems here is that the devil doesn't get to keep Christ! To solve that one, some theologians came up with the "bait-hook" model: Christ came as a human being (the bait), and the devil snapped at the bait but ended up with the hidden hook—Christ's divinity, which allowed Him to escape the devil on resurrection morning. However, later theologians had difficulty accepting the idea that God deceived the devil at the Cross. Even though the devil has no "right" to be treated fairly, God must be righteous in everything He does.

So we come to Anselm of Canterbury.* In his model, it's not Satan who receives the payment of Christ's blood on the Cross. Rather, it's God the Father who does. Anselm's theory, often referred to as the *satisfaction theory*, reflected the contemporary feudal culture, in which society was organized around feudal lords and serfs and in which crime was highly personal—an offense against the feudal lord. Criminals must either suffer punishment or provide *satisfaction*. The latter was very similar to the Catholic concept of doing penance—the satisfaction didn't necessarily have any direct relationship with the sin committed or its punishment.

Anselm applied that concept to his model of the atonement. God is the lord of the universe. Sin is an offense against God and His honor, and the laws of justice in the universe demand that the penalty for so serious of an offense be death. However, there is an alternative. One can provide a "satisfaction" that will satisfy the honor of God and allow Him to forgive the offense to His honor and dignity. "So, then, everyone who sins must repay to God the honour that he has taken away, and this is the satisfaction that every sinner ought to make to God."[3]

---

*Anselm (c.1033-1109) was a bishop in France and then the archbishop of Canterbury in England. He wrote a famous book, *Cur Deus Homo?* ("Why did God become man?"), in which he presented his theology of the incarnation and Cross of Christ as a dialogue between two characters.

The problem, of course, is that none of us can provide a satisfaction equal to the gravity of our sin against a holy, sin-hating God. Only Someone greater than us, greater than our sin, could provide an adequate satisfaction. The answer is Christ. God Himself provides His own "satisfaction." Christ was incarnated, and, as a human being—as our substitute and representative—died in our place. God's honor is satisfied, and we are forgiven and saved.

While variations on this satisfaction model have arisen during the thousand years since Anselm, it is still essentially the orthodox understanding of the Cross and the atonement. It has been called the "penal substitution model" because in it Christ's substitution satisfies the penalty that God imposed. It is called "forensic" and "legal" because it focuses on the payment and transaction metaphors—justification and redemption. We sin, end up guilty in court, and the court must be "satisfied"—someone must endure the punishment. Christ endured the punishment in our place, and the Judge lets us go free. It is called the "objective" theory of the atonement because it makes God the "object" of the Cross. God is the audience; the Cross is for the Father. It is to satisfy His honor, pay the price that He demands for sin, pay the penalty He decreed at the Tree back in the original garden. Because this model in all its variations focuses on God as the One whom the Cross must address or satisfy, it can be referred to as a "God-centered" theory of atonement.[4]

MORAL INFLUENCE THEORY/PETER ABELARD

The major alternative model has been the one most often associated with Peter Abelard (c. 1079-1142), who at one time was a student of Anselm. Abelard included some of the traditional concepts of the atonement, but his emphasis differed greatly from that of Anselm. Abelard didn't believe anyone had to die in order for God to forgive sins. He said God has forgiven for thousands of years (see Psalm 51). Christ forgave on the Cross and asked the Father to forgive before He died.

Neither did Abelard feel that God was so worried about His "honor" that He required "satisfaction"—through death, no less—for offenses against it. Nor did he believe that God was bound by some laws or rules of justice. Nothing is higher than God. God makes the rules!

Abelard believed that the "problem" was not God's offended honor, but humankind's loss of understanding and appreciation of God's love. The problem is not with God but with human brokenness, human alienation from God. So, Abelard concluded, what people needed was a new and greater revelation of God's love, which would break and melt their hearts and draw them back to a personal relationship with God. Here's a sample of what Abelard said:

> Christ . . . has demonstrated to us that supreme love of which Christ himself speaks: "Greater love has no one than this" (John 15:13). We are thus joined through his grace to him and our neighbor by an unbreakable bond of love. . . . Therefore, our redemption through Christ's suffering is that deeper affection in us which not only frees us from slavery to sin, but also wins for us the true liberty of sons of God, so that we do all things out of love rather than fear.[5]

This view is often known as the *moral influence theory* because it focuses on how the Cross influences us, drawing our hearts back to God and thus breaking the power of sin. It is also known as the "subjective" theory of the atonement because, instead of focusing on God as the object and focus of Christ's sacrifice and on heavenly records and accounts that "objectively" need to be dealt with, the Cross is instead God focusing on human beings—on the inner, subjective hearts of sinners. It is not records that need to be pardoned through blood, but inner hearts that need to be healed. It is labeled "exemplarist" in that Christ comes as an *example* of God's love and grace. It is representative of more human-centered theories of the atonement.

Abelard's model quickly met with a negative reaction. He was eventually excommunicated (perhaps for other factors as well). And still today many theologians reject this model, charging that it does away with substitution and minimizes the necessity of the Cross of Christ.

The debate over these two models has raged for nearly a thousand years. God has used each model to draw people to Him. Proponents of each model can point to texts that support its emphasis: Those in favor of the objective model (Anselm's) point to all the texts that refer to ransom, payment, propitiation, etc., and those who prefer the subjective model (Abelard's) point to all the texts that speak of God demonstrating His love to us through the Cross.

The objective model provides a great sense of relief. It says that all our debts have been paid, so we stand free before God. We have been liberated; the record books of heaven have been expunged of the record of our sins. Supporters also believe that it defends a "high" view of sin—our sins are so great that only the sacrifice of God Himself could "satisfy" the penalty's demands. And this model fits the substitutionary concepts so clearly stated in Scripture.

However, the subjective model has its strengths too. It speaks warmly of the love of God. It resonates with our sense of brokenness, the loss of relationship because of the Fall in the Garden. It fits what we know of life and psychology—that people sin because of a psychological need, because of some damage in the past. And it affirms the healing power of true, unconditional love. The plan of salvation is not about cleansing heavenly accounts, but healing the damaged human soul. God is not a bookkeeper, but a doctor—healing the human heart, setting people free from their past to live godly, fulfilling lives.

Each view has also suffered some hits. The objective model seems to divide the Trinity—one member has to "kill" the other in order to forgive. It seems to have a harsher picture of God—God is so worried about His offended honor that He has to establish an extreme penalty for a single sin—eternal death, inflicted by Himself. It seems to make God subservient to a system of higher laws of justice. And it seems to say that the problem that must be solved, the Being who must change, is God, while the evidence of our own conscience and numerous texts indicate that the central problem is with us, not with God. He is perfect, righteous in everything He does (Daniel 9:14). He never changes (Malachi 3:6; Hebrews 13:8). How could the Cross somehow make God "better" or more loving and merciful than He already is?

On the other hand, people have also made a number of objections to the subjective model: It seems to slight the entire concept of substitution and doesn't satisfactorily explain exactly *how* the Cross of Christ revealed God's love if it was not in some way substitutionary. It doesn't demonstrate how Christ's death is more efficacious or effective for us than any other tragic death; for example, that of Gandhi. In this model the Cross seems of little help to those who never had a chance to "see" its revelation of God's love because they never heard the gospel. From this perspective, how was Christ's death "for them" in any meaningful sense? And many say that it's "soft" on sin, that it suggests that sin is merely a psychological problem that needs to be cured, rather than a terrible offense against the sovereign God of the universe.

VICTORY MODEL/GUSTAV AULÉN

A third model, often associated with Gustav Aulén,[6] has been offered as an alternative. Aulén claimed that this view was actually the "classic" atonement theory, though many scholars wouldn't agree. This model says the world came under the dominion of Satan and his demonic forces. Eventually, Christ had to come into the enemy camp and defeat Satan *mano a mano* in a cosmic battle for supremacy. Christ "fought" him first in the desert, second by living a spotlessly pure life, and third by dying and then rising triumphantly from the grave. On the Cross, Christ decidedly defeated Satan and all his demonic hordes and assured the eventual triumph of God's kingdom over evil.

I lived in Chicago during the peak of the Michael Jordan years, when the Chicago Bulls, the NBA basketball team on which he played, won six world championships. Over and over again Jordan would come down and shoot the winning basket as time ran out. Of course, whenever he won, all the Bulls won. And all eight million of us living in the Chicago area strutted around, proclaiming ourselves the world champions of basketball. We had done nothing—except to be fans of the greatest player in the history of the game.

The victory model says that when Christ won that cosmic battle, we all won. It's a very powerful model and has meant a lot to millions of us. And it has broad and significant scriptural support, from Genesis 3:15 to Revelation 12.*

But theologians have pointed out weaknesses in this model too. Most problematically, it doesn't clearly and adequately explain how the victory on the Cross works *for us*. How does Christ defeating the enemy somehow translate to freedom for us—does it simply inspire us to our own victory over Satan?

REVELATORY SUBSTITUTION

So, what to do? Every model has its strengths and its weaknesses. Can we find a model that combines the strengths from several and has few serious weaknesses? Here is the model that comes closer than anything else I've seen to satisfying these criteria:

---

*See Colossians 2:15; Hebrews 2:14, 15; Luke 4:18; John 12:31; 1 John 4:4; Revelation 12:10-12.

1. God is the only Source of life in the universe.

2. God placed a test at the Tree that would help Adam and Eve learn this reality. Passing that test would express their love and loyalty to God, while also solidifying their commitment to Him.*

3. God's warning at the Tree was a loving warning of the natural consequences of sin, rather than a threat of divine punishment. God is not worried about His "honor." He is not subservient to any laws outside of or higher than Himself. This was simply reality, and the eternal future of their relationship was dependent on their realizing that cause-and-effect reality.

4. Satan's attempt to win Adam and Eve away from God was consistent with his lies in the war in heaven, which questioned the goodness and character of God.

> God was represented as severe, exacting, revengeful, and arbitrary. He was pictured as one who could take pleasure in the sufferings of his creatures. The very attributes that belonged to the character of Satan, the evil one represented as belonging to the character of God.[7]

Satan questioned God's goodness and fairness in creating a tree with magnificent fruit and then forbidding Adam and Eve from enjoying it (Genesis 3:4). He also questioned the statement that they would surely die if they disobeyed God, using his own continued existence as proof. He implied that God was the kind of God who would withhold the very best.

5. Adam and Eve sinned, eating fruit from the Tree. Their sin wasn't primarily the act of eating the fruit. It wasn't primarily transgressing a code of restrictions. They doubted God's goodness and

---

*In that sense, the test was not arbitrary or bad news. To be expressed, love must have choices. That test confirmed their love. It confirmed it not only to God, but to themselves.

love, which led them to disobey Him. This doubt, this lack of faith, lies at the root of all sin.

6. Once Adam and Eve sinned, the problem was not sins recorded in the record books of heaven. The problems were (a) their distrust of God's love, goodness and fairness, which needed to be restored; (b) the loss of a personal, face-to-face, continual, healing relationship with God; (c) their doubt that God's warning, "If you sin, you will surely die," was actually true.

7. God's solution had to address these three problems. He could have either Adam or Eve die the second death. That would immediately teach the surviving person that sinners will surely die, but it would cut the class in half. *You can learn about the consequences of stealing with a little bit of jail time—but you can't learn about the consequences of sin with a little bit of death!*

And if God had executed either Adam or Eve, the one left behind and all the other beings in the universe would have had reason to question God's love and goodness. He would have been perceived and related to with fear: "If you mess with God, He'll destroy you." "He says, 'Love Me, or I'll kill you.' "

8. So, God had to underline the fundamental reality of the natural consequences of sin in such a way that (a) Adam and Eve could be kept alive to be able to learn the lesson; (b) they would be convinced of His love, grace, goodness, truthfulness, and fairness; (c) He could have a personal, face-to-face relationship with them again.

9. The incarnation of Christ was the ideal solution. By living among the human race, Christ could reveal Himself through His life and His teaching, and through the Cross and the Resurrection. And, as a substitute, He could die in humanity's place to demonstrate the natural consequences of sin.

10. So Christ promised to come (Revelation 13:8). He came as a baby, giving up, for a time, His use of His divine powers (Philippians 2:5-8). He came to show how to serve God without fear (Luke 1:74).

He revealed God perfectly (see Hebrews 1:1-3; John 17:2-5).

11. He entered the Garden, where He took on, vicariously, the sins of the entire world.* He literally felt the guilt of every sin ever committed. And what did He feel? *Separation.* The natural consequences of sin. It wasn't the Father that was crushing out His life. The Father wasn't killing the Son. The Father and Son, in absolute unity, experienced the separation together.[8]

> The guilt of every descendant of Adam was pressing upon His heart. The wrath of God against sin . . . filled the soul of His Son with consternation. All His life Christ had been publishing to a fallen world the good news of the Father's mercy and pardoning love. . . . But now—[9]

What would you expect the rest of that partially quoted sentence to say? Doesn't it sound like a lead-up to a contrast—that while previously Jesus had known God's mercy and love, now, as He bears our guilt, He's going to experience God's wrath and condemnation? However, that's not what follows. The rest of the sentence says: "But now with the terrible weight of guilt He bears, *He cannot see the Father's reconciling face*" (emphasis supplied). God hasn't changed! He is still "reconciling"—still full of mercy, grace, and pardoning love. Sin has caused no change in God. He hasn't gone anywhere. The change is in Jesus; He lost His sense of the presence of the Father, due to sin. That is the natural consequence of sin.

12. Christ dies on the Cross. He is our Substitute. On the Cross, the entire universe can see these three lessons:

(a) Sin kills. It destroys. It will eventually crush out your life. But not at the hand of God. God didn't kill Christ. The fundamental reality of the universe is that God is the only

---

* Read the chapter entitled "Gethsemane" in White, *The Desire of Ages.*

source of life. So, regarding Satan's accusation in the Garden, it is now clear that God is the truth (John 14:6) and Satan is a liar. Even the unfallen angels had their last questions answered (see Colossians 1:20, 21; Revelation 5:11, 12).

(b) God is a God of love (John 3:16; 1 John 4). He is not arbitrary. He does not angrily destroy sinners. Any parent can immediately see the depth of the love that moves a person to sacrifice an only son, a beloved son, so that others might live.

(c) The "door" to God's heart has been opened once and for all. The veil into the Most Holy Place, the throne of God, was ripped from top to bottom. Christ said, "I have set before you an open door" (Revelation 3:8).

SUMMARY

The great blessing of this model is that it preserves all that is positive about the character of God. It preserves all our nonnegotiable anchor points. And it locates the sin problem that the Cross needs to solve where it should be—with us, not with God. He never changes. Nothing separates us from His love (Romans 8:38, 39). Matthew 5:43-48 clearly shows that God's love is absolutely constant, unchanging, and perfect; He loves even His enemies, even sinners. The Cross didn't have to change God; God can't love us any more than He already does! God was in Christ reconciling *the world* to Himself. He hadn't gone anywhere. It was the prodigal son, not the father, who was lost. Maybe the clearest verse on this point is Jesus' ringing statement: "I, when I am lifted up from the earth, will draw all men to myself" (John 12:32). This verse powerfully indicates that Christ Himself saw the purpose of the Cross as drawing the whole world back to God. He clearly saw the Cross as a gift to His Father, but the gift was in giving a lost world back to the Father.

The other great positives in favor of this model are as follows:

- Like the objective model, this model makes substitution foundational. And it keeps the cold-eyed acknowledgment that sin is pervasive and corrosive and that its consequences are terrible—sin destroys people.

- Like the subjective model, it recognizes the need all humans have for healing from the damage of sin. And it focuses on the incredible love of God, showing that the central goal of the Cross was to win the hearts of lost people back to friendship with God, to persuade them to trust His love.

- Like the victory model, it preserves the theme of the cosmic controversy between Christ and Satan. However, it puts greater emphasis on the fact that the controversy is about truth in contrast to the questions and doubts that Satan has spread ever since the initial rebellion in the hallways of heaven. It also provides the reasons why *Christ's* victory gives *us* victory.

- This model avoids the weaknesses of the objective model. It focuses on human beings, not God, as the problem. It preserves the unity of the Trinity. The Three Persons do what They do absolutely together. When you see One, you see the Others. God's justice and His love don't contradict each other. He is absolutely integrated—all His thoughts and character traits are moving towards the same goal!

- This model preserves the morality of God. His demands for the penalty for sin are not beyond what any human parent would wish. It's consistent with our belief that God is morally superior to all parents and loves His children more.

When I first began to wrestle with the challenging questions about how the Cross and atonement work and why Jesus had to die, I wondered how I could be a Christian with the Cross as the absolute center of my faith if I couldn't explain them. I was terrified that I might never get to the bottom of a theology of the Cross that answered all objections and was faithful to all the evidence. While this conflict was raging inside me, I went to the "Glory of Easter" drama at the Crystal Cathedral. The angels swinging overhead, the camels coming down the aisle, and the incredible music mesmerized me. The great Easter story built to the pivotal moment when Christ was hoisted up on the Cross, the spike was placed on the arch of His foot, and the huge sledgehammer came slashing down on it. The clang of that hammer smashing against that spike penetrated deep into my heart.

I settled something that night. I decided that whether or not I could ever master the theology of it all, I was never, ever, giving up on the Cross. Clearly, something happened there at the Cross that took care of the sin problem. And so I worship the Christ of the Cross while I continue studying the meaning of the event.

1. White, *Desire of Ages*, 83.

2. For clarification on the mixture of the divine and human in inspiration, see White, *Great Controversy*, Introduction, and idem, and *Selected Messages*, (Hagerstown, Md.: Review and Herald, 1958), 1:16-23.

3. Anselm of Canterbury, *Cur Deus Homo?* The Library of Christian Classics (Philadelphia: Westminster Press, 1956), 10:119, quoted in Jack Provonsha, *You Can Go Home Again* (Hagerstown, Md.: Review and Herald, 1982), 29.

4. See L. W. Grensted, *A Short History of the Doctrine of the Atonement* (Eugene, Ore.: Wipf and Stock, 2001).

5. Provonsha, 30, 31; McGrath, 426.

6. Gustav Aulén, *Christus Victor* (New York: Macmillan, 1969).

7. Ellen G. White, *Signs of the Times,* January 20, 1890.

8. McGrath, 278.

9. White, *Desire of Ages*, 753.

EXCURSUS B

Q: How does the model you've given differ from the moral-influence theory, which was "discredited" so long ago with the excommunication of Abelard?

A: This model overlaps with the moral-influence theory only in that it is a human-centered theory of atonement—it says that human beings are the primary ones who need a Cross. Here's how it avoids the weaknesses of the moral-influence theory:

First of all, it preserves substitution at the center of the model. It does adjust the focus of the substitution from changing God's heart to changing human beings' hearts, to teaching certain realities and truths to a sinful world. But substitution is still crucial and necessary. People complain that the moral-influence theory does not make clear exactly *why* the Cross of Christ demonstrates the love of God more than does the death of any other tragic figure. This model attempts to do just that.

Second, this model portrays God as dealing with *all* the results of sin. Sin is not just a list of offenses in the record books of heaven, and it's not just a deficit of love in sinners or a lost and broken relationship with God. Our theology of the atonement must take care of those issues, but the father of lies has also raised questions, and each of these lies must be answered in order for heaven and the new earth to be eternally safe.

(1) Satan questioned the reality of God's statement that sinners would surely die. The Cross definitively answered that question—sinners do surely die. God knows that for eternity to be safe, every

inhabitant of heaven is going to have to respect "reality," the laws of cause and effect. These are laws not because God designates death for sin but simply because this is reality: God is the only Source of life in the universe, and those who separate from Him lose life eternally.

(2) The Cross demonstrates clearly the true cost of sin—what it does to the sinner and what it does to God. Christ, as our substitute, demonstrated what sin does to people as He went through the emotional devastation of losing contact with the Father, which the wicked experience in every sin and will experience fully at the end of the world. Christ also demonstrated what sin costs God—separation, Godforsakenness. He gave up His Son at the risk of eternal loss—what an unbelievable gift! [1]

(3) Satan suggested that we have to fear God and distance ourselves from Him because He is the kind of God who will destroy us if we cross Him in the slightest. Christ's unforgettable cry that God was "forsaking" Him, not killing Him, on the Cross answers that question. If God destroys sinners, then God would have had to kill Christ, proving Satan right. But God did not kill Christ. Christ emphatically stated that He would lay down His own life (John 10:17, 18). He stated that God doesn't take life (John 10:10). And Matthew 27:46 makes it clear that God was forsaking Christ, giving Him up, rather than killing Him. So, Christ made it clear that we never have any reason to fear God. Fear the terrible, natural consequences of sin, yes—but not God!

(4) The Cross demonstrates the full and total Oneness of God. The Trinity stand absolutely together in everything they do. Sin threatened their historic Oneness—but even in that extremity Christ turns repeatedly to the Father: "Forgive them," "Take this cup," "Into Your Hands I commit My spirit." They were still together by faith, if not by "sight."

(5) At the Cross, God's love was linked with forgiveness. Jesus and the Father were forgiving the world through the Cross. Jesus

freely forgave the thief on the cross. He was not begging an angry, vengeful God to reverse Himself and forgive. He and the Father were demonstrating before the universe that They are forgivers at heart. They need no "blood" to be persuaded to forgive. The blood was Their demonstration of the incredible extent to which They were willing to go to communicate Their love and forgiveness to anybody, including Their "enemies." When Jesus offered forgiveness to the very people killing Him, He highlighted the very core of the Cross— God is a forgiver, and the Cross was His most powerful way of communicating that forgiveness.

(6) Many other systems of religion require the seekers to provide some sort of offering, sacrifice, prayers, and/or rituals to propitiate the deity, to satisfy the gods, to gain merit for themselves or for their loved ones, including the dead. The Cross cuts across all such pagan systems.

David made it clear: "You would not be pleased with sacrifices, or I would bring them. If I brought you a burnt offering, you would not accept it. The sacrifice you want is a broken spirit. A broken and repentant heart, O God, you will not despise" (Psalm 51:16, 17, NLT). God doesn't need or want sacrifices. God isn't the One who needed to be changed. It's the human heart, not God's, that needs to be changed, broken, and made repentant. Certainly God has asked for sacrifices—but only as they pointed forward to the *gift* He provided on the Cross.

Notice how J. I. Packer, a Reformed theologian, links the Cross and the traditional penal substitution model to the changing of God's verdict from a No to a Yes:

> Christ's death had its effect first on God, who was hereby *propitiated*. . . . The thought here is that by dying, Christ offered to God what the West has called *satisfaction* for sins, satisfaction which God's own character dictated as the only

means whereby his "no" to us could become a "yes." . . . By undergoing the cross, Jesus expiated our sins, propitiated our Maker, turned God's "no" to us into a "yes," and so saved us.[2]

However, if God's heart never changes and His answer to sinners is always "yes" (as this book is suggesting, see the next chapter), then the Cross *must* point in a different direction than that pictured by theology like Packer's. God cannot be the primary audience of the Cross—we are! This is so important because of what it implies about God—that sin changes God's attitude toward sinners. How can we claim that God's love never changes and at the same time suggest that His vote changes from "yes" to "no" the moment we sin?

Therefore, the Cross was far more than just an attempt by God to convince us of His love through the tragedy of the Cross. It was His masterstroke, His grand design to teach huge truths—to nail down the answers to the most basic, fundamental questions of existence, and to do so in the most powerful, dramatic, magnetic, heartbreaking, and heart-touching way possible.

1. See Ellen G. White, *Education* (Nampa, Idaho: Pacific Press, 1952), 263.

2. J. I. Packer, "What Did the Cross Achieve? The Logic of Penal Substitution," *Tyndale Bulletin* 25 (1974), 3-45, quoted by Alister E. McGrath in *Christian Theology: an Introduction*, 3rd ed. (Blackwell), 425.

EXCURSUS C

Q: What about the metaphors?

A: Remember that each metaphor has strengths and weaknesses and, if pressed too far, can distort the truth about the character of God. The metaphors serve most helpfully when we take the best of each of them to form a composite that portrays the Cross as the greatest event in salvation history.

Ransom: Yes, we have been kidnapped. Yes, we need Someone Else to make the ransom payment—to liberate us. But we press the metaphor too far when we picture God paying Satan or Christ paying and satisfying the demands of His own Father.

Justification: Yes, we have sinned; we're guilty, condemned. And we need the Judge to set us free, to vindicate us, to declare us guilt-free before the universe and our own accusing conscience. And the goal is to place us in a justified relationship with God, resting and trusting in His unchanging love, as if the sin had never occurred. But we press this metaphor too far if we have God demanding eternal death as the penalty for a single sin. We distort the point if we focus primarily on expunging record books in heaven, rather than focusing on the need for the healing of a personal relationship with the Father and the healing of our inner soul and our relationships with others.

Reconciliation: Yes, we have been separated, alienated from God. Our relationship with Him has been broken, and we are incapable of restoring that relationship by ourselves. But the Bible clearly indicates that it is always God who initiates the reconciliation

(2 Corinthians 5:18, 19). Christ reconciles us to God, not God to us. God's heart didn't need "blood" in order to be reconciled!

Redemption: Yes, we are slaves to sin. Yes, we need Someone outside ourselves to redeem us, to set us free. But we go too far if we imply that Christ had to make a payment to the slaveholder (Satan) in order to set us free.

Accounting: Yes, we owe a debt (Matthew 18:21-35; Romans 4:1-8). Yes, it's more than we can pay; we need Someone else to pay it for us. Yes, we have been bought with a price. And, yes, sin is certainly a dishonor to God. But we must be careful about considering the blood of Christ payment to a demanding God.

Sacrifice: Yes, God deserves our entire life. Yes, we are called to be sacrifices to Him. And yes, Christ was just such a sacrifice (Ephesians 5:2). But that sacrifice was not to change the heart of God. God announced at Christ's baptism that He was already totally pleased with Christ. The Cross did not improve His regard of Christ. Here again we have to be careful of paganism, which says people must offer sacrifices to appease and propitiate a bloodthirsty god. God was not in heaven refusing to forgive until He saw Christ complete the sacrifice.[1]

---

1. White, *Steps to Christ*, 13.

CHAPTER FIVE

Grace, Hell, and the Unchanging God

When Dan Rather, the CBS evening news anchor, was a young college student down in Texas, he worked part-time at a one-man radio station, playing records and doing the news, the weather, sports—everything. To have time for a meal, he would put on a thirty-minute LP album of a sermon, race to the local restaurant, and race back.

One day he put on a Baptist fire-and-brimstone preacher, raced into town, raced back, spun into the gravel parking lot—and saw the owner's car there. As he entered the studio, the owner shouted at him, "Where have you been? Do you know what's been happening?" Turns out a scratch in the record had the Baptist preacher shouting over the plains of Texas, ". . . go to hell! . . . go to hell! . . . go to hell!"

Hell is the ultimate question—how to avoid going there, whatever hell you believe in. Every religion wrestles with this question.

C. S. Lewis walked into a meeting of his fellow philosophers when they were discussing what constituted the central difference between Christianity and the other world religions. Lewis is reported to have said, "That's easy—it's grace!"[1] Our answer to what makes the difference between going to hell and going to heaven is always and only grace. Our motto at the La Sierra University Church is *Grace—Everyone, Everywhere, and Every Time.*

Grace, Hell, and the Unchanging God

Is God always, immediately, perpetually, and constantly gracious? Or does He at times withhold grace, offering it only when we meet certain conditions? In other words, does His grace at times depend on factors outside of Himself, or is He gracious all the time, no matter what we do?

Recently I have been asking the questions this way: Is God the constant, or is He the variable? Is God the One who decides who's going to be saved and who's going to be lost?—is He the variable? Or do *we* decide, which makes us the variable? To use J. I. Packer's language, is God's answer sometimes No and other times Yes, or does He always say Yes?

The belief that ultimately God decides who will go to heaven and who will go to "hell" allows several options. Let's take a look at them:

Universalism: God is so gracious that He will hold the door open long enough and find enough creative ways to forgive and heal that eventually everyone will be saved. God decides, and He is a constant; He chooses for everyone, and everyone will be saved.

Predestination: Augustine and the Reformers taught that Christ's death is always "effective," meaning that everyone for whom He died has to be saved. But some will not be saved, so Christ must have died only for the "elect"—people chosen beforehand to be saved. Christ made a limited atonement. If you don't believe in universalism, but you believe that God makes all the decisions and does all the work, then double predestination is the only option left. God decides, but He is the variable; He chooses for everyone—some to be saved and some to be lost.

Legalism (or righteousness by works): God sets the standard (the constant), but the people do the works. They're the variable; some (most) will not be saved.

Penal substitution: Still the most popular theology of the atonement, this has God as the variable. When people sin, He is forced to withdraw His salvation and forgiveness. His honor is offended; His Yes becomes a No. People's names are removed from the Lamb's book of life. They are "lost." But when people accept Christ as their substitute, then God is satisfied again. His requirements have been met, and, to repeat Packer's phrase, God's No! becomes Yes!

GOD IS A CONSTANT

As I have wrestled with this over the years, I have moved toward the view that the Scriptures, taken as a whole, show God as a constant. He is perpetually gracious. His love is unconditional. He is forever faithful. Nothing we do changes His attitude toward us in the slightest. In our relationship, God is the constant and we are the variable.*

Here are some of those Scriptures: "I the LORD do not change" (Malachi 3:6). "Jesus Christ is the same yesterday and today and forever" (Hebrews 13:8). "I am convinced that neither death nor life, neither angels nor demons, neither the present nor the future, nor any powers, neither height nor depth, nor anything else in all creation, will be able to separate us from the love of God that is in Christ Jesus our Lord" (Romans 8:38, 39). In the last quotation, Paul clearly and directly says that *nothing* ever separates us from the love of God. We can certainly separate ourselves from God, but nothing we can ever do or not do makes the slightest difference to the heart of God toward His "children."

Jesus is unmistakable about this in His famous Sermon on the Mount: "Love your enemies. . . . He causes his sun to rise on the evil and the good, and sends rain on the righteous and the unrighteous. . . . If you greet only your brothers, what are you doing more than others? Do not even pagans do that? Be perfect, therefore, as your heavenly Father is perfect" (Matthew 5:43-48). People have used this latter passage to support perfectionism. However, the context is clear—

---

*This is far from cheap grace or "once saved, always saved" or eternal security, as the rest of the book will make abundantly clear!

Grace, Hell, and the Unchanging God

Jesus was talking about love! Our love is supposed to be like God's love, which never changes! He loves even His enemies. There is no switching from Yes to No and back again. He's always Yes!

And Jesus clearly contrasts this with pagans, who love based on external factors, on behavior. They love only their friends, those who are like them, or those who love them back. Not God! And not Christians. God's love is consistent, inexorable, and irrevocable. Agape love. It is never "love if" or "love because" but only "love, period."

Other texts make it clear that God's love is universal and inclusive: "God so loved the world" (John 3:16). God is "not wanting anyone to perish" (2 Peter 3:9). "He is the atoning sacrifice . . . for the sins of the whole world" (1 John 2:2).

For years, starting with my very first class in Romans in college, I struggled with the unfairness of it all. We had no choice in getting stuck with the consequences of the first Adam's sin, but we have to make a choice in order to benefit from the consequences of Christ's sacrifice on the Cross. It didn't seem fair!

In the past few years I have read it differently. The gospel is fair! Romans 5:18, 19 indicates that in the same way that sin has come from one man and brought sin, condemnation, and death involuntarily to all humankind—so, in the same way, by His sacrifice on the Cross, Christ has brought grace and forgiveness and eternal life to all humankind!

God is a constant! The atonement is not limited. The Cross has shown us the Father's heart—it is a constant. He has already loved and accepted and forgiven everyone for all their sins, past, present, or future. All anyone has to do is to not *reject* that forgiveness and grace, and they will have eternal life (Hebrews 2:3).

There are always two aspects to forgiveness—God's part and our part. When we say that in Christ, God has already forgiven all the sins that have been or will ever be committed, we are talking about God's part. We still have to accept the forgiveness. When we say that

God has already poured out His grace to everyone, we are talking about God's part. When we say that God justified the entire world at the Cross, we are referring only to God's part. Millions will be lost—but they will be lost by their own choice, even though they're forgiven, justified, in God's heart.

Some have been troubled about the concept that all have already been justified in Christ at the Cross. Justification simply means that God treats them as "justified"—"just as if they've never sinned." It means that His Yes has never turned into a No. They are forgiven. They are loved just the same. Nothing has ever changed on God's part, in God's heart. Being justified and being covered with grace are just other ways of saying that God's love never changes. "It"—God's provision for their salvation—"is finished."

This has absolutely nothing to do with "once saved, always saved!" People can certainly reject salvation. God's forgiveness will only truly and ultimately benefit those who respond to Christ with faith. But it must be very clear that as far as God is concerned, His forgiveness is settled and has been settled forever. The Cross didn't change God's heart. It *is* the heart of God. Sin is heartbreaking to God, but it never changes His heart for His children.

This is why the New Testament contains texts such as "This grace was given us in Christ Jesus before the beginning of time" (2 Timothy 1:9). "The Lamb that was slain from the creation of the world" (Revelation 13:8). "Now a righteousness from God, apart from law, has been made known, to which the Law and the Prophets testify" (Romans 3:21). "It is by grace you have been saved, through faith—and this not from yourselves, it is the gift of God—not by works, so that no one can boast" (Ephesians 2:8, 9).

These last two texts are very clear. God's grace is never based on anything we do. God's grace is a constant! It doesn't come and go. It is not off and on. "See, I have set before you an open door" (Revelation 3:8). "[Love] keeps no record of wrongs" (1 Corinthians 13:5). "All

Grace, Hell, and the Unchanging God

this is from God, who reconciled us to himself through Christ . . . that God was reconciling the world to himself in Christ, not counting men's sins against them" (2 Corinthians 5:18, 19). This is all past tense—it's already happened! We never have to do anything to reconcile God to us—God has already reconciled us to Himself through Christ.

An old golf pro died a few years ago—Harvey Penick, 90 years old. He had taught some of the great players. He wrote down his ideas in a little red notebook. Someone suggested that he get it published. He sent it to some publishers. One wrote back, saying that they would love to publish it for an advance of $90,000. Penick wrote back that he and his wife were old, with a lot of medical bills, and they just could not afford $90,000. The publishers wrote back, saying, "No, the $90,000 isn't something you give us—the $90,000 is something we give you!" With God as a constant, the gospel is not something we do for God or something Christ did for God—it is something God did for us. "It is finished!" Done.

The story of the prodigal son (Luke 15:11-32) makes it abundantly clear that the Father's love is a constant. Nothing the son did or didn't do could ever change the father's heart. He stood watching and waiting for the son to return. When the son did return, he didn't say, "Show me the money!" He didn't ask for an apology. He ran, he opened his arms, he welcomed his son back, and he threw a party. Here, in what may be the defining story of Christ's picture of His Father, God is clearly a constant. His love and grace and mercy are absolutely locked in, forever and ever.

And King David's sins are no secret—murder, adultery, and lying. As a result, he and his family suffered huge natural consequences. But look at what God said! "As Solomon grew old, his wives turned his heart after other gods, and his heart was not fully devoted to the LORD his God, as the heart of David his father had been" (1 Kings 11:4).

Did God forget? You can't sin any worse than David did! And yet God said David was fully devoted, that he kept all His laws and did

71

not fail to keep *any* of the commands—except in the case of Uriah (see 1 Kings 3:6; 11:33; 14:8; 15:5).

Did God forget? No! God is a constant! He had so totally forgiven and justified David that it was as if none of David's sins had ever happened. That is the reality in the heart of God. "Wash me, and I will be whiter than snow" (Psalm 51:7). "You are accepted before God just as if you had not sinned."[2]

THE IMPLICATIONS

Sin: The view I grew up with was that sin changed God's attitude. I was in trouble with God. I was going to have to perform certain steps: repentance, confession, prayer, making things right, offering the blood of Christ to God, and then God would decide whether or not to forgive and reinstate me. This new view suggests that *sin doesn't change God—it changes me,* changes my heart, my soul. It doesn't distance God from me, it distances me from God. God never moves; we move away from God.*

Forgiveness: I always understood that in order to be forgiven, I first had to do all those steps, and *then* God might be persuaded to forgive! This turns it around—*God's forgiveness is always first, always prior.* It is His forgiveness that leads me, draws me to confess (Jeremiah 31:3; 1 John 4:19). Our faith is always a response to His grace, which is a constant and never dependent on any of our actions or attitudes.

Atonement: Our sins certainly make God ache for the pain we cause ourselves and others. But contrary to Anselm's position, *our sins never cause such a dishonor or offense to God that He feels He is forced to withdraw His love, grace, and forgiveness.* He never switches from Yes to No. The Cross was never meant to switch God's vote. It was to announce to us God's eternal *Yes!*

Prayer: Prayer is the subject of a later chapter, but I'll introduce the major thesis here. Many Christians believe that prayer changes

---

*This will be explored further in the next chapter.

Grace, Hell, and the Unchanging God

God. They think that getting God to decide to intervene in response to our requests requires many prayers and many people praying and the holiest people praying. Isn't it clear already, though, that if God is a constant, prayer is never meant to change His heart! It has many other profound purposes—but it is not meant to persuade God to be better than He already is. He is perfect! He is righteous in all that He does (Daniel 9:14). It is impossible to make Him more willing to save, to intervene. There are important "great-controversy" reasons why He has to restrain His power today. But the reasons are *never* that He is unwilling. God's love is a constant; we are the variable!

Judgment: (Again, more about this in a later chapter.) The traditional view of the judgment has God hearing our case in the cosmic courtroom of the universe. Our name is called out, the record of our life is read out loud for all to hear, and then God decides whether we will be saved or lost. God is the variable!

However, quite a number of texts say that God has already judged! He has already justified the world, given everyone grace and forgiveness. He is the constant; we are the variable. It is we who decide whether or not to accept Him. He stands outside the door knocking, waiting for our answer (Revelation 3:20). He knocks on every door. He wants to come in to all. "God did not send his Son into the world to condemn the world, but to save the world through him. Whoever believes in him is not condemned, but whoever does not believe stands condemned already because he has not believed in the name of God's one and only Son" (John 3:17, 18).

There is a wonderful old legend about a princess kidnapped from her father's palace. For years her father sent servants to search the kingdom for his daughter. One day a servant recognized her. He stopped her and told her who she really was. Gradually, the sense of her true position in life returned. She was always and forever the princess—she just needed to recover her awareness of that reality. That's our situation. We have already been saved and justified; we just haven't realized it. We need to recover the realization that we are already children of God and an incredible inheritance is ours!

Paul wrote of "God who justifies the wicked" (Romans 4:5). Justification is a present reality; God treats us as justified, just as if we had never sinned. But it is also a last-day, eschatological judgment; He has already justified the wicked, already forgiven them eternally. It's settled, finished! We simply must forego rejecting it all! God has silenced the accuser of the brethren once and for all (Revelation 12:10-12).

John 10 pictures Jesus as the Good Shepherd. It also warns of false shepherds. Jesus says that His sheep know His voice; when He calls, they will follow. When the false shepherds call, those who don't know Jesus' voice will follow the false shepherds. It's not the heart of God, but whether the sheep know the right voice that makes the difference. God is a constant; *we* are the variable.

GO ON IN!

Queen Esther decided to go before the king to try to save her people even though by doing so she would make herself subject to the penalty of death for breaking the law that no one should enter the king's presence without his invitation. She stood outside the door, wondering whether the king would extend the scepter to her. Finally she walked through the doors into the throne room—and the king extended the scepter to her. She would live; she would not die.

That's the gospel that the young Ellen Harmon heard a Methodist minister preach.[3] He said too many people are standing outside the door to the throne room of the God of the universe, afraid to go in. Go on in! Inside you'll find a gracious God.

In Queen Esther's story I see four points regarding salvation: First, Genesis 49:10 contains a messianic prophecy in which the scepter represents Christ. Esther had to wonder whether the king would extend the scepter to her or not. We don't have to wonder! Christ has already been extended to us at the Cross, once and for all.

Grace, Hell, and the Unchanging God

Second, if Christ is the scepter, who is the king? The king must be God the Father. Too many people are much more comfortable with Christ than the Father and see Christ as more willing to save than the Father—Christ has to go "intercede" with the Father. No! The Father is exactly like Christ (John 14:9; Hebrews 1:3). "The Father himself loves you" (John 16:27). It is the Father who offers Christ to the world.

Third, we don't offer Christ to the Father—the Father offers Christ to us (2 Corinthians 5:18, 19).

And finally, once God has extended the scepter (Christ), He *never* takes it back. God is a constant! His love, grace, acceptance, and forgiveness are constant—immovable forever. He knows everything about us, yet nothing we do affects His attitude toward us in the slightest. The scepter is always out. The door is always open. It is finished. Settled. Once and forever.

In every other relationship in life, if you don't perform, if you don't compete, you'll suffer negative consequences. You'll get fired, you'll lose the game, you'll lose the girl. In only one relationship in the universe does our behavior *never* affect how the Other relates to us. And incredibly, that relationship is the one that determines our eternal destiny! That's what grace is all about: *Grace—everyone, everywhere, every time!*

In an interview, Meryl Streep was asked, "If there is a God and you get to heaven, what do you hope God will say?"

She replied, "Everyone's in!"

That's exactly what God says. Only those who refuse to go in are lost. Everyone who *wants* to be in *can* be in. God is a constant!

---

1. Philip Yancey, *What's So Amazing About Grace?* (Grand Rapids, Mich.: Zondervan, 1997), 45.

2. White, *Steps to Christ*, 62.

3. See the story of her conversion in Ellen G. White, *Testimonies for the Church*, volume 1 (Nampa, Idaho: Pacific Press, 1948).

CHAPTER SIX

Grace, Works, and the Good Life

Bruce Larson said that every time a pastor preaches, half the audience needs the opposite sermon! When pastors preach a powerful message of grace, someone warns about "cheap grace" or "once saved, always saved." People fear that the preaching of radical grace will leave some feeling no need to live sanctified, God-honoring lives.

On the other hand, when pastors preach a strong message about sanctification, holiness, victory, the Ten Commandments, or church standards, those fearing cheap grace cheer the preaching of "the straight testimony." But others—those who have struggled with guilt all their lives, who never feel good enough, who struggle with the thought of living up to all the rules—leave discouraged. The load they're already carrying has grown heavier.

Let's try to find some balance.

REAL GRACE *ALWAYS* CHANGES LIVES

"We are God's workmanship, created in Christ Jesus to do good works" (Ephesians 2:10). "God's grace alone can work a reformation."[1] "It is His grace that gives men power to obey the laws of God."[2]

Someone gave me the video *Pretty Woman* to watch, telling me it's a contemporary version of the Bible's story of Hosea. While I'm certainly not recommending the movie, it does come pretty close to the Hosea story: A man takes a prostitute from the street to a penthouse suite. He gives her a credit card so that she can go shopping for the best clothes on Rodeo Drive. By the end of the movie they have fallen in love. And the grace she experienced has healed and changed her at the core of her being, and she refuses to be used as a prostitute ever again. The way she was treated on the outside (justifying grace) has healed her on the inside (sanctifying grace). Real grace always changes lives!

Just because we're saved by grace is no reason to be stupid! In her book on the Ten Commandments, *Smoke on the Mountain,* Joy Davidman, C. S. Lewis's wife, compared God to a life guard who rescues a drowning swimmer. "But," she said, "you can't drown all the time!"[3] There comes a time when we want to live mature, godly, healthy lives—when God has set us free to be all that we can be.

Some ways of doing life are just better and more fun than others. When we're forgiven and our record is clean and our sins have been deleted and we're OK with the God of the universe—why would we then screw up our life by doing things that we know will damage and cheat us of the best of life?

When Solomon was installed as the new king, God asked him what gift he most wanted.* Solomon asked for wisdom. God was so pleased that Solomon requested wisdom rather than riches or power that He gave Solomon all of them. Solomon had so much gold that he had his smiths create five hundred golden shields to hang on the walls of the temple. Whenever he had grand ceremonies, his servants would polish the golden shields. The sunlight would glisten on them, and everyone would know of the blessing God had given Solomon and the children of Israel.

Then Solomon began to compromise. Foreign gods. Too many wives. And his empire began to crumble. His son Rehoboam followed him as king and was even worse—crueler, more rebellious

---

* I got the idea for what follows from a magnificent sermon by Dr. Benjamin Reaves.

against God. Eventually, God allowed the Egyptians to take all the treasures from the temple, including all the golden shields. Rehoboam had no more gold, but he had plenty of brass. So he had his smiths make five hundred brass shields. He hoped that if they polished the brass shields, in the grand ceremonies the sun would glisten on the brass and the shields would look like gold and no one would know that the gold was gone. He had traded the gold for brass.

That's what so many have done with their lives. God has given them gold. He has given them talents, great families, good education, church, mentors, everything. So much potential. And it's spoiled. They let an enemy come in and steal the golden shields from the soul temple of their hearts, and they've tried to replace it with brass.

Here's the point: *The problem with sin and compromise is never what it does to God; it's what it does to us. It cheats us!* The consequences of sin are natural and intrinsic rather than unnatural and extrinsic! Solomon had so much potential. Think of what he *did* accomplish, and then try to imagine what he and his descendants *might* have accomplished had they chosen to stay true to God throughout their lives, to not fritter away their potential the way they did.

Sin doesn't damage God. Nor does it change His heart. God is a constant! Sin damages us, our souls, and the people we love most.

GOOD WORKS

Let's look again at the role of good works in the Christian's life.

1. Our salvation is never based on our good works. God's love is a constant; His door is always open. You can always go home again. He always forgives. The worst sins don't faze the love of God in the slightest. Yes, we will show our faith by our good works—but those good works will *never* become the basis for our salvation. Our best works— even good works done by God *in* us—are tainted by our humanity.[4]

I lived in Chicago during the best Michael Jordan years, so I use a lot of Michael Jordan parables! Let's say that during Michael Jordan's prime years as a basketball player he was killed in a car accident and his body was then frozen. Suppose someone let me have his legs, and I had them transplanted onto me. Suddenly, I'm six feet, six inches tall. I shave my head. I buy Air Jordans. I buy a red shirt with the number 23 (Jordan's number) on it. I try out for the Bulls. I can jump forty-eight inches high now, so I can dunk. But I can't shoot. I figure it must be the right hand, so I go back, have another surgery—get his right hand. Now I can shoot the lights out. But somehow by halftime I'm always exhausted. Must be the lungs. So I go back and get his lungs. But when I get back on the court, I can never seem to figure out what to do, where to go. Must be the brain and the eyes. So I go back and get Michael Jordan's brain and his famous, piercing, competitive eyes. Now I've got it all. I'm the best. I'm all over the court. I can do it all. Until the end of the game. Whenever we get to the end of the game and they want me to take the last shot to win, I just can't do it. I'm too scared. I never make it. It must be the heart. So I go back and get his heart!

You get the point: No matter how much of Michael Jordan I get, as long as there is anything of me still in there, I will never be Michael Jordan! That's why our salvation has to be all Christ. Nothing of us. All a gift. All grace. "Fear God, and give him glory" (Revelation 14:7).

2. We live godly lives in response to God's grace. "I urge you . . . in view of God's mercy, to offer your bodies as living sacrifices" (Romans 12:1). It honors God when we respond to His incredible, amazing grace by living pure, victorious, godly lives.

3. God knows best. Here's the heart of it: Satan's original temptation to Eve was to doubt what God had said. God said those who ate the forbidden fruit would die. Satan said, "No, you'll be as gods." To be a follower of Christ is to decide that God knows best. Disciples of Christ take Scripture totally seriously. Jesus said, "The words I have spoken to you are . . . life" (John 6:63). Bill Hybels, the pastor of the

Willow Creek megachurch, says, "I have scars in my life as a result of failing to follow the teachings of Scripture." I think we could all say that. God knows best.

4. God wants the best. Not only does God *know* best, He *wants* the best. "I know the plans I have for you, . . . plans to prosper you and not to harm you, plans to give you hope and a future" (Jeremiah 29:11). "Taste and see that the LORD is good" (Psalm 34:8). "The thief cometh not, but for to steal . . . : I am come that they might have life, and that they might have it more abundantly" (John 10:10, KJV). God doesn't steal anything good from us. He gives life.

5. Living a godly, righteous life honors God and draws people to Him. While living the moral life doesn't purchase our salvation, it honors God, glorifies God, and draws people to Him (Matthew 5:16). People learn about God's love through our love (1 John 4:8-12). We are to be the "aroma of Christ" to the world (2 Corinthians 2:14-16). People learn a lot about God's character from other people. We are the ones who make God look good "on the street"—in real life.

The third commandment says, "Thou shalt not take the name of the LORD thy God in vain" (Exodus 20:7, KJV). That covers far more than four-letter words! God's name stands for His character. Third-commandment people (especially those who are also fourth-commandment people!) have such a passion for God that they would rather die than misrepresent God in any way. They hate sin (Genesis 3:15). They refuse to use any of the "weapons" of the world: anger, lies, power plays, gossip, subversion (John 18:36). They bring every thought captive to Christ (2 Corinthians 10:3-5). They will be the nucleus of the 144,000 who have the name of the Father and of the Lamb emblazoned on their foreheads (Revelation 14:1). They tell "no lie" about the Father (Revelation 14:5).

God said that Job had "spoken of me what is right" (see Job 42:8).

Grace, Works, and the Good Life

Godly people want to live so that God can say that about them. As we lift Christ and the Cross up, we draw people to Him (John 12:32).

6. In the long run, the godly life is the most enjoyable, richest, most creative, and most fulfilling life possible. Daniel and his three Hebrew friends absolutely refused to compromise. They refused to eat the king's food and came out ten times smarter. Daniel's friends refused to bow down to the king's image, and they had the privilege of experiencing the miracle of Christ meeting them in the furnace, and they escaped with not one trace of fire on their clothes. After the edict requiring residents of Babylon to pray only to the king, God watched to see what Daniel would do when he went home. When Daniel passed the closet, threw open the window, and prayed aloud as he always did, I think God said, "Yes!" Daniel was true-blue his entire life, and God blessed him and made him prime minister of two pagan world empires. We don't have to cut corners to get ahead.

A few years ago, climbers found the body of George Mallory near the top of Mount Everest. He was a British climber who disappeared on Everest in 1924; he may have actually reached the top before Sir Edmund Hillary. Someone called Hillary and asked how he would feel if it was discovered that he wasn't the first. He said he wasn't losing any sleep: "Getting down is important, too!"

It doesn't matter how high we go in life, how much money we make, how much short-term pleasure we enjoy—if we lose out on eternal life in the process. We must look at our whole life when making decisions about which lifestyle will be the most fun and the most fulfilling.

7. Living the godly life is the best way to avoid pain. When God does make restrictive laws, it is to help limit pain in our lives. Living a righteous life is certainly no guarantee that we'll be spared pain and suffering in this life. But one of the most powerful motivations to live a righteous, godly life is to avoid the natural consequences that sin brings. People who live righteous lives may not avoid all cancers, but by not smoking they may avoid lung cancer. We can avoid jail, getting someone pregnant while unmarried, or killing someone by driving while intoxicated.

When we choose the "natural consequences" interpretation back at the Tree in the Garden, then we see the consequences of sin as being primarily intrinsic rather than extrinsic. Then we won't avoid sinning because we don't want to make God angry or to avoid being lost. Rather, we'll avoid it because we don't want to damage our life or cheat our potential. We don't want to trade gold for brass.

Dorothy Sayers noted the difference between stop-sign law and fire law:[5] When the village council puts up a stop sign at an intersection, people who roll through it get a ticket and have to pay. If the council votes to take down the stop sign, people can roll through the intersection without penalty. But if the most powerful government in the world were to vote to do away with the law of fire, those who test their new "freedom" would soon discover that fire still burns.

The Ten Commandments are *fire* laws, not *stop-sign* laws. They are not arbitrary commands chosen by God to test our loyalty and obedience. They are laws that protect us from the pain of natural consequences. It makes just as much sense to follow these moral laws as it does to follow the laws of gravity and motion.

8. God ultimately wants His laws written on the heart. It seems clear that God never meant for the Ten Commandments and all the other laws and counsels to have to be codified, spelled out in detail, and shouted from the top of Mt. Sinai. We're told that when the angels first heard the Ten Commandments, the revelation that there was a law "came as a thing unthought of."[6] The very essence of heaven was love. All the needs of its inhabitants were met. Living a righteous, loving life was instinctive. There was no need for a handbook, for laws to be spelled out in heavenly assemblies. Angels spoke

Grace, Works, and the Good Life

truthfully and worshipped naturally, freely, without coercion, pressure, or fear. Everything they did made eminent sense and was obviously exactly the best thing to do.

When God had to spell out detailed moral instructions to Adam and Eve and their descendents and warn them of the consequences of disobedience, He must have found it heartbreaking. That was an accommodation because of sin. All the rules were absolutely consistent with His character and with the nature and atmosphere of heaven—but having to spell them out was just a loss. God should never have needed to shout or to use thunder, smoke, and lightning. But it evidently was the only way to get the attention of people coming out of four hundred years of slavery, to preserve their lives long enough to teach them the intrinsic value of obeying His laws. (We will pursue this further in the next chapter.)

Under the new covenant, God wants us to return to His original intention—the way it was in heaven and the way it will someday be again. When we pray, "Thy kingdom come, Thy will be done," we are praying for the power and freedom to live by the values of the heavenly kingdom today.*

"This is the covenant I will make with the house of Israel after that time, declares the Lord. I will put my laws in their minds and write them on their hearts. I will be their God, and they will be my people" (Hebrews 8:10). Paul repeatedly calls Christians to live a life of freedom. "Where the Spirit of the Lord is, there is freedom" (2 Corinthians 3:17). Some have misinterpreted that as freedom from God's laws. While we are certainly free from the *condemnation* of the law and from the tyranny of trying to be saved by the law, God still calls us to live godly lives, guided by the values of the Ten Commandments. But as we grow in Christ, as the laws are written on our hearts by the Spirit, living the godly life begins to feel free and natural. "God ain't heavy."

---

*In theological language, the church lives "proleptically"; that is, we anticipate the future kingdom in our life today.

Jesus said, "My yoke is easy and my burden is light" (Matthew 11:30). We have thought through our values and have bought in to the wisdom of living by God's will, whether it's expressed in the Commandments or in Proverbs or in the Sermon on the Mount. We have been convinced of the truth of Jesus' promise, "My words are life."

Alden Thompson, professor of Old Testament at Walla Walla College, has developed a famous pyramid chart that illustrates this process.[7] At the bottom are all the various specific laws and instructions given in Scripture. These rules are applications in time and place of the Ten Commandments, the next level up. Moving further up, we find Jesus' summary of the Ten Commandments: the two laws of love—love God and love your neighbor (Matthew 22:37-40; Leviticus 19:18; Deuteronomy 6:5). And of course, these two can be summarized by a single law—love.

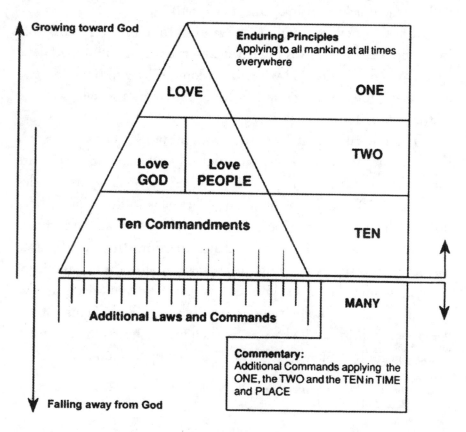

Thompson's point is that the higher we go up the pyramid, the more natural our moral life feels and the more "free from the law" we feel—not because we are living contrary to God's laws, but because the laws are so ingrained in our soul as the richest way to live that we almost never have to make reference to the actual, specific codes. There is "enmity" against sin (Genesis 3:15). The fruit of the Spirit grows naturally (Galatians 5:22, 23; John 15).*

There's an area on the clubs, bats, and racquets used in sports known as the "sweet spot." When you hit the ball with that sweet spot, it feels lighter and livelier than it does when struck anywhere else. That's how the normal, godly life should feel. When we aren't fighting God's will, it all makes sense to us.

9. Guidelines to "church standards." If anything has led people away from the church and caused them to get a jaundiced view of the character of God, it has been conflict with "church standards." Here are a few guidelines that I try to follow in teaching on this prickly topic:

• *The standards must make absolute sense* (Isaiah 1:18). They must clearly contribute to the abundant life rather than stealing from it (John 10:10).

• *The standards should feel easy and light rather than difficult and burdensome* (Acts 15:19; Matthew 11:28-30; Deuteronomy 30:11-15).

• *The standards must focus on principles rather than specifics.* When the delegates to the 1980 General Conference session in Dallas wrote

---

*"All true obedience comes from the heart. It was heart work with Christ. And if we consent, He will so identify Himself with our thoughts and aims, so blend our hearts and minds into conformity to His will, that when obeying Him we shall be but carrying out our own impulses. The will, refined and sanctified, will find its highest delight in doing His services. When we know God as it is our privilege to know Him, our life will be a life of continual obedience. Through an appreciation of the character of Christ, through communion with God, sin will become hateful to us." White, *Desire of Ages*, 668.

the church's twenty-seven fundamental beliefs, they left out some of the traditional "church standards" that were not expressly stated in Scripture, such as prohibitions against theater-going, dancing, and gambling. They replaced them with biblical and Christ-centered principles that can apply in every age and to every contemporary situation.

• *The standards must be personal.* No choice is moral unless it is personal. If we "act moral" simply for the sake of convention or the rules of the school or our work or the government, rather than because of our personal, internalized free choice, then we fall far short of what God considers morality.

Someone said to me, "I'm sorry that, as a pastor, you have to live so carefully." I replied, "Please don't feel sorry for me! I live exactly the way I want to live." If I thought I could have more fun living some other way, I would do that. I choose this life. I don't look at someone else's pornography and say, "Sure wish I could look at some of that." I don't watch people who are drinking beer and wish I could have some. My virgin strawberry daiquiri's fine; I don't want to need some chemical to feel good, to get a high.

We reach the highest levels of moral development when we transition from living for external authorities to living for internal ones, when we make personal, intentional moral choices (see the next chapter for more on this topic). When we don't care who's watching or how far we are from home or whether it is day or night, but live by our choices—period. That's when God's laws truly are written on our hearts.

When I was on a mission trip to the Philippines one year, the plane that was supposed to take us home didn't arrive, so we had to transfer to another city to catch a different flight. Unfortunately, our luggage went a different direction, so at one o'clock in the morning I was on the sidewalk in front of our hotel waiting for it to catch up with us. A young man came up to me, showed me pictures of young girls, and said, "You want chicks?" I suppose I could have gotten away with it—I was eight thousand miles away from home and everyone else was asleep. But I'm not doing that. I'm not dishonoring God, my wife, my family, my church, or myself like that. And it's my choice. I like my life just this way.

It is absolutely the right and responsibility of parents and educators to control the moral lives of young children. But that control must never be confused with true, meaningful moral character. Only when people are making moral decisions personally and individually, based on a set of values that they have thoughtfully studied and chosen—only then are those moral decisions meaningful. Only then do they bring glory to God.*

10. Our good works must be related to Christ.

• *Real change is possible only through Christ.* "If anyone is in Christ, he is a new creation" (2 Corinthians 5:17). "I can do all things through Christ, who strengthens me" (Philippians 4:13, NKJV). I used to tease my church by telling them that I was going to put up a basket in my backyard—put it low enough that I could dunk the basketball. I said I would practice ten dunks every day and raise the basket an inch a day until I could dunk like a basketball star. But it wouldn't work. I could practice from now until eternity, and I'd never be able to dunk the ball! But the gospel says I can be like Christ: "We, who with unveiled faces all reflect the Lord's glory, are being transformed into His likeness, with ever-increasing glory, which comes from the Lord, who is the Spirit" (2 Corinthians 3:18).

---

*God has designed the maturation of young people to happen over an extended time while they are growing up. During that time they work through specific developmental tasks, including differentiation and individuation from the lives and values of their parents and societal institutions. Any time we retain control beyond the transitions designed by God, we risk creating rebellion. Wise parents, teachers, and pastors/church leaders must remain extremely sensitive to this sequence of transitions.

• *I want nothing to keep me from Christ.* Have you heard the old story about the balloon man? He carried a big bunch of balloons everywhere he went. At the fair, he entered a drawing for a free cruise, and he won! He took a taxi to the ship; squeezing all the balloons into the taxi wasn't easy, but he made it. As he got on the ship, everyone else had balloons too, but when the ship sailed, they let theirs go. He kept his; he's the balloon man!

When it was time for dinner in the elegant dining hall, he could smell the delicious food. But he couldn't get through the hallway with all the balloons, so he settled for cheese and crackers on the deck. And when it was time to go to his stateroom for the night, again, he couldn't make it because of the balloons. So he wrapped a blanket around himself and slept on a deck chair.

Every day was the same—cheese and crackers and blanket on a deck chair. Finally, on the last day of the cruise, he received an engraved invitation to eat dinner at the captain's table. Oh, how he wanted to go. All day he agonized. What was he to do? Finally he went to the back of the ship, unclenched his fingers, and let the balloons go. He watched until they were out of sight. Then he went to his stateroom and dressed for dinner with the captain, where he had the best night of his life!

As Oswald Chambers has said, "Beware of anything that competes with loyalty to Jesus Christ."[8]

• *I want to live my life as a gift to Christ.* "When you think of what he has done for you, is this too much to ask?" (Romans 12:1, NLT)

When I was a youth pastor in Portland, Oregon, some people invited my wife and me to their home for dinner after church. We were to bring a cherry pie. We had to stop at someone's house on way there, so my wife put the pie on the floor of the car while we made our visit. When she got back into the car, she forgot about the pie and put her foot right in the middle of it! We picked it up and brushed the dirt off, but the footprint was clearly visible! We couldn't fix it, and, of course, we didn't have time to bake another pie. So we drove on to our hosts' home, walked up to the front door, and handed them our pie with the footprint in it and told them what happened. Terrible! (We ate the pie anyway!)

I don't want to walk into the gates of heaven with my life marred like that. Because of what Jesus has done for me, I want to give Him the gift of my life. I want it to be the very best gift I can make it. By His grace. Because of His grace. To honor His grace.

---

1. White, *Testimonies,* 4:378.

2. Ellen G. White, *God's Amazing Grace* (Hagerstown, Md.: Review and Herald, *1973),* 103.

3. Joy Davidman, *Smoke on the Mountain* (Philadelphia: Westminster Press, 1954), 14.

4. Ellen G. White, *Selected Messages* (Hagerstown, Md.: Review and Herald, 1958), 1:344.

5. Dorothy Sayers, *The Mind of the Maker* (San Francisco: Harper & Row, 1941), 4ff.

6. Ellen G. White, *Thoughts from the Mount of Blessing* (Nampa, Idaho; Pacific Press, 1956), 109.

7. Alden Thompson, *Inspiration: Hard Questions, Honest Answers* (Hagerstown, Md.: Review and Herald, 1991), 115. Used by permission.

8. Oswald Chambers, *My Utmost for His Highest* (Westwood, N.J.: Barbour Books, 1963), 18.

CHAPTER SEVEN

Hard Questions About the Old Testament

For thirty years, I have been tormented by hard questions about the Old Testament: Why in the world did God have to turn Lot's wife into a pillar of salt just for looking back to see her home being destroyed? Why did Uzzah have to die just for trying to keep the ark from falling over? Why didn't God have the Israelites punish just Achan and the Amalekite warriors instead of having them kill the women and children too? When He gave the Ten Commandments, why did He have to shout and throw in the thunder, smoke, and lightning? Why did He have she-bears maul forty-two young people just for teasing Elisha about his bald head? And why would He punish people "unto the third and fourth generation" (Exodus 20:4-6)?

Many people think the Old Testament pictures God as trying to control people or as eliminating all His competitors or as destroying people who messed with Him. They think it says that when people sin, He becomes angry, and people have to sacrifice lambs and even children to calm Him down. They think that the bad things that happen come from God because people sinned. If people didn't live right—keep all the rules—the ground opened up and swallowed them or He sent a flood or had people stone them and their kids and even their dog. With fasting and hundreds of nitpicky rules, He took the fun out of the Sabbath.

And after all that, God had the gall to say, "Delight yourself in the Lord." I want you to love Me, with all your heart, with all your soul, and with all your mind. Millions of "seekers" have turned away from Christianity or at least found it difficult to draw close to God because of this picture of Him.

So, what are we supposed to do? We believe the Bible is inspired, and we want to love God. But we're stuck with these stories that don't seem to fit the picture of God in the rest of the Bible. We have emphasized over and over again that God is a constant—God is One, the Trinity cannot be divided against Themselves. There are certain nonnegotiable anchor points about God—He is love; He is good news; He refuses to use fear to coerce; He doesn't want a master/ servant relationship with us, but rather one of friends. How does this other picture of God square with all these stories?

Before you decide that the easy answer is to forget the Old Testament and stick with the New Testament, don't forget Ananias and Sapphira being punished with instant death for not bringing in *all* the money from the sale of their property (Acts 5). How can the Bible say "perfect love casts out fear" when God does that to people because they didn't pay enough tithe and offerings? And don't forget the book of Revelation, the very last book of the Bible, which should give the clearest and most exalted picture of God. Revelation contains some of the Bible's roughest passages—read the third angel's message in Revelation 14:9-12 again, in case you've forgotten what it actually says!

Millions have accepted the traditional model. They believe that God's wrath will be poured out on sinners for even one single sin. But, they say, His grace leads Him to direct His wrath against His own Son instead. Most Christians also believe either that God will burn people in hell, working a miracle to keep them alive so He can torture them forever, or that He commits His "strange act" (Isaiah 28:21) and destroys them all with fire, though they're burned up quickly. How can we square all that with this other picture of God as characterized by love?

SOME ANSWERS

Here are some options that have been suggested:

1. Just live with the tension. As one lady said angrily about all this, "Why try to fix it? That's just the way God is. He's the only God we've got, so just live with it!" Her model suggests that we have to live with a picture of God that mixes love and nit-picking and that we have no business in trying to force God into the boxes that we like. God is free to be whoever He is—He's God! And He is a God who can both love us in Christ and be incredibly harsh and destructive against sin and perversion. It says the truth lies in the absolute balance of the "hard" and "soft" sides of love. This view has the advantage of accepting every text and quotation at face value; each bears the same weight and makes the same contribution to truth.

2. We can divide the Trinity. Gnosticism, a heresy in the early church, developed a model that pictured the Creator, the Old Testament God, as harsh, and Christ, the Logos/Word, as filled with grace, light, and love. Many people since have perhaps unconsciously accepted a form of this, being much more comfortable with Jesus Christ and the New Testament than they are with the Father of the Old Testament. Christ is Christmas and Easter and grace and love and the gift of eternal life. The Father is the Judge, the Lawgiver, the One who threatens and punishes and destroys. However, Christ was explicitly clear that He and the Father are exactly alike, and Hebrews 1:3 states that Christ is the "exact representation of his being."

3. We can consign one set of passages to a category below "inspiration." If the two sets of passages are mutually exclusive, then one set must not be truth and therefore not as inspired as the other. Obviously, this flies in the face of the Bible's claim that "all Scripture is inspired." But many have chosen this option and decided that those who wrote the biblical passages that don't conform to their preferred model were simply giving their own opinion.

4. We can reinterpret all the "love" passages in terms of the harsh. If we are going to accept that all Scripture is inspired, then we must see if one model can explain all the inspired material. Perhaps the love and grace passages can best be explained in terms of the Bible's harsher, "justice" passages.

5. We can reinterpret all the harsh passages in light of the love passages. Rather than interpreting the love passages in terms of the harsh ones, we can try to develop a model that views the love passages as the best explanation of the harsh passages. This method preserves the nonnegotiable anchor points we've studied. And it preserves the authority and inspiration of Scripture. But it's also controversial because on the surface it appears to subordinate some texts in favor of others, and those who hold it can be accused of forcing an external agenda onto the Bible, selecting only the texts that fit what they already believe and ignoring or twisting the rest to fit that preconception.

For the past few years, I have taken as a personal challenge the attempt to find principles of interpretation that would relieve some of the tension in Scripture. My goal has been to find, from within the Bible itself, a method of interpretation that will integrate all the biblical material about God into one cohesive, consistent picture, without damaging the inspired text. Here's what I've hammered out for myself and collected from others as I've wrestled with this dilemma.

PRINCIPLES OF INTERPRETATION
1. We have to acknowledge the diversity that Scripture contains. Some passages very clearly indicate that God is love and grace and noncondemning (1 John 4:16, 18; John 3:16; 8:11; 10:10; 15:15; Jeremiah 31:3; Hosea 11:8; Matthew 11:28-30; Romans 8:1, 38, 39). At the same time, all the passages listed earlier contain stories in

both the Old and New Testaments that appear to picture a God who is almost pagan and brutal in His acts of vengeance and punishment.

2. We accept and believe in the inspiration of all sixty-six books of the Bible, Old and New Testaments, and take it all seriously as the Word of God. We believe that the truth we are seeking is found in the composite picture of God developed throughout the entire canon of Scripture. We refuse to ignore any part of Scripture simply because it doesn't fit our preconceived ideas about God that come from our postmodern culture or somewhere else.

3. We believe it is possible to develop a picture of God that does justice to every passage and story. If one doesn't fit, it is because we haven't understood it yet! The type of tension we're discussing in this chapter exists in virtually every doctrine the church has developed; it hasn't made us discard the doctrines of the trinity, the state of the dead, Christology, the Sabbath, law and grace, etc. Neither should it keep us from developing a consistent picture of the true character of God.

4. It is not only permissible but actually mandatory that we give certain scriptural concepts and themes priority over others. It is on this point that this subject gets complicated and controversial, but bear with me and see what Scripture itself says. Here's the key passage: "In the past God spoke to our forefathers through the prophets at many times and in various ways, but in these last days He has spoken to us by His Son, . . . the radiance of God's glory and the exact representation of His being" (Hebrews 1:1-3).

The basic thrust of this passage seems very clear: God first spoke through the prophets but eventually felt that it was still necessary to send Christ Himself. If it was necessary to send Christ—God Himself—as the *exact* representation of His being, then, clearly, the earlier witnesses must not have been "exact." Evidently a witness can be inspired, called of God, and canonical—but not be as "exact" as the witness of Christ Himself.

It is hard to imagine how any could argue with this. It is the essence of Christianity to believe that Christ is God's last word. Scripture says: "No one has ever seen God, but God the One and Only, who is at the Father's side, has made him known" (John 1:18). "Anyone who has seen me has seen the Father" (John 14:9). "I and the Father are one" (John 10:30). "God . . . made His light shine in our hearts to give us the light of the knowledge of the glory of God in the face of Christ" (2 Corinthians 4:6). The fact that at the crucifixion the temple veil ripped from top to bottom, thus offering a view into the Most Holy Place for the first time, also implies that something unique and unprecedented had happened (Matthew 27:51).

So, it seems necessary, based on an absolutely foundational belief about the uniqueness of Christ, to affirm that some revelations of God are clearer than others—and to say that this affirmation doesn't damage our doctrine of inspiration.* Can any Christian dispute the statement that Christ is the clearest picture of God this world has ever seen? That's basically what it means to be a Christian—to believe that God is exactly like Christ. And if Christ is the clearest picture of God this world has ever seen, then the other revelations are less clear. They are inspired, and they are profound, and they are truth—but they are not *as clear* as Christ. They are lower-case "t" truth compared to His capital "T" Truth.

In 1982, the *Adventist Review* published a seminal series of articles entitled "From Sinai to Golgotha" written by Alden Thompson.[1] Essentially, Thompson said that God inspired Bible writers throughout history, but Christ is the clearest picture of God and

---

*I call this concept "vertical hermeneutics," as contrasted with more traditional "horizontal hermeneutics." Rather than having every text speak equally, vertical hermeneutics establishes a hierarchy of authority within Scripture, with Christ always being the last Word.

truth and therefore must be the controlling and defining factor in all exegetical interpretation of the Bible. Some struggled with this concept. If God is perfect, doesn't it follow that everything He inspires must be equally perfect? How can one passage or book be more perfect than another?

The answer lies in the incarnational nature of Scripture. In the same way that God joined human and divine natures in the incarnation of Christ, Scripture also joins the human and the divine. Human men were inspired with God's revelation, with God's truth. Because human beings grow and learn, it seems logical to expect that the longer prophets serve, the more they grow in the depth of their knowledge and understanding of God and His truth. That would imply that what they wrote at the apex of their prophetic career would be clearer and more profound than what they wrote earlier. Everything they wrote would be inspired and useful, but their later writings would present the mind and ways of God more clearly, closer to the "bull's eye" of capital "T" Truth.

Ellen White seems to teach this concept directly when she affirms, "For sixty years . . . I have been constantly learning in reference to divine things."[2] In fact, there is an entire genre of study in which a prophet's writings are analyzed chronologically to see where they have grown and matured in their understanding of what God has revealed to them. Anyone who reads the writings of Ellen White will notice the greater maturity and depth of her picture of Christ and of God in the books written during the later stages of her prophetic ministry: *Desire of Ages, Christ's Object Lessons,* and *Thoughts From the Mount of Blessings,* etc.

There are several reasons why we should expect some variation within Scripture: (1) The growing maturity of the prophet. (2) The uniqueness and superiority of the witness of Christ as God Himself; the pure, unadulterated, pristine revelation of God. (3) The teaching process God would naturally use in growing the understanding of

His people, starting with the "milk" of the Word and progressing to the "meat" (Hebrews 5:12-14).

5. Love is the ultimate guiding value, controlling all descriptions of God. Sometimes, in the thick of a debate about a theme in Scripture, one side accuses the other of bringing an outside agenda to the Bible and arbitrarily giving certain texts or ideas priority over others. The Bible itself establishes this priority. The clearest example is "love." The Bible says loves overrides everything else. Love is the default. Everything ultimately has to be resolved in favor of love. "These three remain: faith, hope and love. But the *greatest* of these is love" (1 Corinthians 13:13, emphasis supplied). " ' "Love the Lord your God with all your heart and with all your soul and with all your mind." This is the first and *greatest* commandment. And the second is like it: "Love your neighbor as yourself." *All* the Law and the Prophets hang on these two commandments' " (Matthew 22:37-40, emphasis supplied). "*God is love.* Whoever lives in love lives in God, and God in him. . . . Whoever does not love does not know God, because God is love." (1 John 4:16, 8, emphasis supplied).

Clearly, then, the Bible itself establishes a "hermeneutical hierarchy." Certain texts, certain themes, were *meant* to dominate others. Love is the greatest; love sums up everything else; everything else "hangs" on love. That means that the primacy of Christ and the primacy of love are determining, defining principles as we try to reconcile all the seemingly conflicted passages about the character of God in the Bible and try to understand the atonement metaphors. This does not contradict or undermine Scripture; it's what Scripture itself demands! Nothing can be stated as ultimate truth that contradicts these two nonnegotiable anchor points.

So, Christ's life of love and His teachings provide ultimate guidelines as to what people should become. The goal is to *be* like Christ, to *think* like Christ. "We, who with unveiled faces all reflect the Lord's glory, are being transformed into his likeness with ever-increasing glory, which comes from the Lord, who is the Spirit" (2 Corinthians 3:18).

6. Creation and heaven represent the ideals that should guide the body of Christ today. We take our ultimate cues from God's original design for life at Creation and from what we anticipate it will be in heaven and in the new earth. Jesus said that His kingdom was not of this world (John 18:36). We have been delivered from this present age (Galatians 1:3, 4) and are already getting a taste of the powers of the age to come (Hebrews 6:5). We are citizens of another kingdom (Ephesians 2:19; Hebrews 11:8–16).

All this means that we cannot regard the stories of violence and vengeance as the last word guiding our ethics. We operate by what we understand to be the ethics and atmosphere of heaven—what God intended His creation to be and what heaven and the new earth will be like someday. These themes take precedence over what we read in the rough-and-tumble of the scriptural world and of our contemporary world.

7. The major themes of Scripture take precedence over isolated texts and/or concepts. This is a time-honored principle of hermeneutics. When we gather all the evidence from the sixty-six books, we try to establish the trajectory of Scripture. What direction does Scripture seem to be headed? We must give that trajectory precedence over isolated texts.

This at times can mean numerical majority. But we can't base our decision on a count of the texts. Sometimes the majority set of texts can be better explained in terms of the minority rather than vice versa. For example, the three or four texts in the New Testament that portray Christ as the Lamb of God control our interpretation of the hundreds of Old Testament texts about lambs.

Related principles of interpretation include the premises that unclear texts should defer to the clear and that symbolic texts should defer to the literal. But the big-picture themes, the cosmic issues, the great events of salvation history, the concepts that clearly have an impact on our salvation must always take precedence over more minor matters (see Matthew 23:23; Romans 14:17).

8. God graciously condescends to speak to people in terms they can understand. This key insight has unlocked much of Scripture for me and released a great deal of the tension I always felt when reading the Bible: *God, in His gracious love and condescension, has often stooped down to speak and to act in terms relevant to and understandable in the contemporary situation.* Many times that has meant He took a huge risk of being misunderstood. And many times that has meant temporarily acting in a way that may on the surface seem out of character. But He has chosen to do it anyway.

The key paradigm here comes from a developmental-stage model, such as Lawrence Kohlberg's stages of moral development. Kohlberg noticed that children move through a series of stages in the development of their moral conscience and motivation. They start with stages one and two, in which punishment and reward are the prime motivators of their behavior. Gradually they mature to stages three and four, which involve more social interaction, but still mean direction by external forces—parents, school, bosses, coaches, government, etc. The most morally mature reach stages five and six, in which their values are internally chosen. Those who reach these stages live by altruism, authenticity, and unselfish love.

As Kohlberg developed his theories, he concluded that individuals halt their progress at a particular level and simply cannot perceive or understand the higher levels at all. It takes certain experiences that jar their equilibrium to bring a breakthrough into the higher stages.

He concluded that 75 percent of the population never move past stage four, Law and Order.*

Now here's an insight I received from Dick Winn years ago: *For God to communicate, He has to speak to people at their level!*[†] God is so sensitive and so multifaceted that He tailors His words and actions to fit the situation exactly. When the Israelites were slaves coming out of Egypt, He had to speak at very elementary levels; that's why He shouted from the top of Mount Sinai! He was willing to "scare" them because He knew it was the only way He could keep them alive until He could bring them along to higher motivations.

We were eating Christmas dinner in Chicago with a group of friends and their families. We were in the dining room, the kids were in the family room, and the kitchen was between, so we couldn't see the kids. Suddenly, one woman completely lost it and started shouting at her three-year-old daughter, "Jerica, you get away from there—right now!" I'd never seen her act like that. Then we found out that the little girl had been putting Christmas wrapping paper into the fireplace, and the fire was following it out into the family room. The mother had no time for a quiet "Jerica, please don't play with fire. We love you; we don't want you to get hurt." She was thirty feet away; she had to shout "Get away from that fire right now!" It was totally out of character for her, and I'm sure she doesn't relate to her daughter that way today, many years later. But at that moment, it was absolutely consistent with love. She did it to keep her daughter alive and the house safe.

So, one major option as a solution to the tension in Scripture is to see God speaking at various levels to various audiences. He speaks in whatever language necessary to get people's attention, to wake them up. He hopes eventually to draw them and mature them to the place where He can speak at the highest levels, the levels of Christ and love, where the laws can be written on their hearts instead of codified on stone.

---

* See appendix, page 204, for a summary of Kohlberg's stages.
[†]Richard Winn, paper done for his doctoral work, private copy in my file.

The classic illustration of God's incredible willingness to descend to our human level is a story about Ellen White and Joseph Bates. Evidently, when Bates first met Mrs. White, he wasn't quite convinced of her prophetic gift. Then one afternoon she went into vision while he was in the room, and in vision she saw planets with moons—first she saw one with four, which Bates recognized as Jupiter; then one with seven (Saturn), and one with six (Uranus). Bates knew astronomy, and he knew that Ellen White did not. So he was convinced of her prophetic gift.

How many moons do we see circling these planets today? Jupiter has sixty-two; Saturn, thirty-one; and Uranus, twenty-seven! But if God had shown these numbers to Mrs. White back in her day, Bates would have disavowed her gift. God showed her exactly the number that corresponded to the knowledge available at that time.[3]

This model says the whole Bible and all Mrs. White's books are absolutely inspired. It also suggests what we should do when we read passages that just don't seem to fit the highest and clearest pictures of God that we've found in Christ. It says that rather than rejecting Scripture or attributing terrible characteristics to God, we should simply applaud His grace in "lowering" Himself to speak in terms people of that time and place could understand.

This solution preserves the authority, inspiration, and integrity of Scripture while also preserving our nonnegotiable anchor points regarding God's character. It allows us to take every passage seriously, searching for why God chose to act or speak in that manner in that situation, and to explore ways of reconciling that with the overall picture of God's character that we find in Scripture. It also allows us to integrate the two seemingly conflicting sets of data about God, understanding one set in terms of the other, but respecting it all.

9. God has, at certain times, used unnatural consequences to teach natural consequences. Here is another key insight that has helped me reconcile some of these challenging Old Testament stories. (I will develop it further in the chapter on prayer and miracles.)

God's miracles are not evenly distributed throughout the scriptural record.[4] We can't assume that God worked miracles every day throughout the biblical era. The miracles recorded in the Bible seem to be clustered around key events in salvation history: the time of the Exodus, the time of Elijah and Elisha, and the time of Jesus and of the apostles and the early church.

Many of us have concluded that God's miracles were not meant to imply that if we simply had enough faith or prayed hard enough or got enough people to pray or lived more righteous lives, God would repeat all the biblical miracles every day in our time. Faith, prayer, and living righteously are all good things to do, but there's no evidence that we could then empty our hospitals and avoid all funerals and walk on water!

The miracles of the Bible can be understood at three levels:

First, the miracles were signs of what is spiritually true today, but physically true at the end of the world. That is when there will be no more pain, no more tears, no more death. That is when the dead will rise and we walk on water, etc.

Second, the miracles were done by one individual, Jesus Christ, as signs of what the entire body of Christ would do in the future. His healings were signs of what the healing gifts of doctors and nurses and hospitals would do in His name. His financial blessings were signs of what the body of Christ has the power to do collectively to care for each other's needs.

And third, the physical miracles were to teach about God's spiritual power. Jesus miraculously fed the five thousand—and then told them that He was the Bread of life and that if they received Him in His Word, they would never hunger again. He healed the blind to prove He was the light of the world, the source of truth.

Now here's the key insight of this chapter: On the positive side, God used *unnatural means* to teach the power of natural choices. In other words, God chose to use very public physical miracles at key moments in salvation history to illustrate the value of using His spiritual power every day. He healed blindness, using unnatural powers, so that we would learn the everyday power of His truth to rid ourselves of spiritual blindness. God took the incredible risk that we would not make the link—that we would assume that if we just had enough faith, we could replicate His physical miracles every day. But He was hoping against hope that we would make the spiritual link. That was the point.

In the same way, on the negative side, God, at pivotal moments in salvation history, stepped in with unnatural consequences to teach about the terrible dangers of natural consequences.

Let me illustrate. As Lot and his family left the burning cities of Sodom and Gomorrah, God told them not to look back. When Lot's wife looked back on her beloved former life, she was instantly turned into a pillar of salt. That seems like a huge overkill for a minor, understandable reaction to leaving one's home and friends and family to live in the mountains. But God wanted to make a huge point— that when He says something as serious as "don't look back," *we must not look back!* We must make a clean break with the past, with the old life. God, with a broken heart, temporarily sacrifices one life, hoping that the story will be told far and wide for thousands of years and save the lives of millions for eternity.

During the Exodus, God, struggling to mold this rebellious group of slaves into a vibrant, alive, spiritual community, uses some very powerful motivations. When He punishes Aaron and Miriam with leprosy, He wants to shout to His people, "Take the leaders I have chosen seriously!" When He allows bears to maul the young people taunting Elisha, He shouts the same message. Each of the stories, if studied long enough, will reveal the same kind of desperate attempt to teach a crucial, life-saving lesson that will benefit millions in the long term.

Some have called these "emergency measures." They were not God's preferred modes of operation. They were God bending down to the level of His people, speaking in terms they could understand, sacrificing a few to save millions. He did this at the risk that we would miss the point, that we would not see the link from His unnatural consequences to the natural consequences of our choices. He took the risk that we would assume that that is just the way God is—if we mess with Him in the slightest, He'll destroy us. Of course, that is just the perception that Satan hopes we will take.

I am suggesting that many of these stories in the Old Testament (and in the New) were God's attempts to speak in stages-one-through-four language—emergency measures, in which God bent down to our level to get people's attention, to wake people up, to keep them alive until He could disciple them to the place where they could see the richness of living at stages five and six, the levels of Christ and love and internalized values of altruism.

God still uses all of Scripture. There are people around the world and in every church at every stage of moral and spiritual development. So, all the stories of the Bible are still relevant. Each of the metaphors about the Cross, though imperfect, still speaks meaningfully to those who need to hear the gospel at their level. Every model of the atonement ministers spiritually to different people.

But God calls us to continue to grow, to mature, to see all of the stories of the Bible and all the metaphors through the lens of Christ. Christ is always the last word on God. He's the ultimate, the fullness of God (Colossians 2:9, 10).

---

1. Alden Thompson, "From Sinai to Golgotha," *Adventist Review*, December 3-31, 1981. The last of the six articles was published in *Westwind*, the Walla Walla College alumni journal, Winter, 1982, 4ff.

2. White, *Selected Messages*, 3:71.

3. Arthur L. White, *Ellen G. White: The Early Years, 1827-1862* (Hagerstown, Md.: Review and Herald, 1985), 1:113, 114. I found updated information regarding the moons at <www.planetary.org/learn/solarsystem/moons.html> and <http://sse.jpl.nasa.gov/planets/index.cfm>.

4. C. S. Lewis, *Miracles* (New York: Macmillan, 1947), 174.

CHAPTER EIGHT

What Really Happened in 1844?

A woman wants to try ice fishing. She reads books about it and gets all the equipment together. Then she goes to the nearest body of frozen water. She gets out her little stool and begins to cut a hole in the ice. Suddenly a voice booms down from the sky, "There are no fish under the ice." Scared to death, she moves down the ice and starts cutting another hole. Again, from the heavens, comes the voice, "There are no fish under the ice." Now she's really scared, but she goes to the farthest point on the ice and tries again. This time the voice shouts, "THERE ARE NO FISH UNDER THE ICE!" She stops cutting, looks up toward heaven, and says, "Is that you, Lord?" And the voice replies, "No, this is the ice-rink manager!"

She thought there were fish there. But she was wrong. Mistaken.

Through the years, many have suggested that our church has been wrong about the investigative judgment. They say that William Miller and the early Adventists were wrong about Christ returning on October 22, 1844, and that we're still wrong in assuming something cosmically important occurred on that day. There are no fish under the ice.

Maybe we are just wrong. What should we do with the investigative judgment: require it, repent of it—or revise it? This has been one of the most controversial subjects in the Adventist Church during my lifetime. It would be far easier to pass by it than to deal with it. However, it has critical implications for the character of God, so let's wade in.

While studying the Bible around the year 1825, William Miller, a farmer in New York state, came to the text: "How long shall be the vision concerning the daily sacrifice, and the transgression of desolation? . . . Unto two thousand and three hundred days; then shall the sanctuary be cleansed" (Daniel 8:13, 14, KJV). He did the math and concluded that the sanctuary would be cleansed in just a few years— the mid-1840s. He assumed that the only place in the universe that needed to be cleansed had to be this world, and so he decided that this cleansing meant that Christ would return to earth on that date.

Miller began to preach about his views and found a large hearing. Eventually, those who accepted his message decided that Christ was going to return on the antitypical day of atonement, which they calculated to be October 22, 1844. Thousands of "Millerites" gathered to await Christ's coming together, fully expecting to be home in heaven with Him by nightfall. It didn't happen. There were no fish under the ice. They had to return to their homes, past their jeering, mocking neighbors. Hiram Edson wrote later, "We wept, and wept, until the day dawn."

Thousands gave up on the whole thing. But a few kept studying. They soon decided that they'd done the math correctly and been right about the date, but they'd been wrong about the event. They began to focus on the cleansing of the heavenly sanctuary and developed the concept that in 1844 Christ went into the Most Holy Place to initiate an investigative judgment. He began going over the books, deciding who would be saved and who would be lost.

OBJECTIONS

Even before the controversies of the late 1970s, many of us had struggled with the basic concept. The quote I had a hard time with was this: "When any have sins remaining upon the books of record, unrepented of and unforgiven, their names will be blotted out of the book of life, and the record of their good deeds erased from the book."[1] I would look around at my relatives, preachers for fifty years, and because I happened to know they weren't perfect yet, I wondered what hope there was for people like me!

Many of us were taught that when we come to Christ and repent and confess our sins, God writes "Pardoned" by our name and our sins, but the record of the sins is still there. When our name comes up in the investigative judgment, our record must be pristine clean, pure white—*and* we must have all our sins totally out of our life at that exact moment or none of our sins will be forgiven, none will be blotted out, and we'll be lost forever. In other words, we have to hope that our name comes up when we're on a hot winning streak or we'll be lost.

Many of us grew up with fear. I was thankful my name started with "S," hoping that God used English and I would have a little extra time before my name came up! My brothers and I were obsessed with the fear that one unconfessed sin would keep us out of heaven if it was on our records when our name came up. We sinned plenty—but we tried very hard to repent quickly, so that our names could not come up before our records were cleared. Many of us grew up staring at Harry Anderson's painting of the judgment—all those steps leading up to God's throne, massive books there, angels with their quills recording everything. Your name comes up, you go out there, and they read all the sins you've ever committed. Monica Lewinsky certainly made a huge mistake—but not many of us would be happy to have our best friend record everything we ever said or did on a hidden recorder. However, that's the picture of the judgment many of us grew up with.

I was a young pastor when Dr. Desmond Ford made his famous Forum presentation in October 1979, at my alma mater, Pacific

Union College. His primary challenge regarding the investigative judgment was that it takes away our sense of security in Christ. It says our sins are not totally forgiven; they're still on the books, when the Bible says that when our sins are forgiven, they're forgotten, sent to the bottom of the sea, separated from us as far as the east is from the west (Psalm 103:12). Ford challenged the idea that the atonement wasn't complete at the Cross, that it wasn't complete until our sins are blotted out from the heavenly sanctuary. How could we have joy and assurance if we're constantly afraid that our name could come up at any time and that if we aren't perfect at that moment, we will be lost forever?

So, how do we meet this challenge? And remember, our concern is for implications about the character of God.

Before we begin answering the challenge, let's remember what qualifications our theology of the judgment must meet. Let's review the relevant nonnegotiable anchor points.

• *It has to be good news:* The first angel's message, which says, "Fear God, for the hour of His judgment is come," also refers to the everlasting *gospel*—everlasting "good news." So, whatever the judgment is, it has to be good news for those in Christ. It has to be such good news that the 144,000, God's final witnesses, are thrilled to go around the world telling everyone about it!

• *Assurance of salvation:* It cannot cause people to lose their assurance of salvation.

• *No fear:* It cannot cause fear for born-again Christians. First John 4:17, 18 clearly tells us that perfect love casts out all fear. If a doctrine causes Christians to fear, then it's wrong.

• *Not ashamed:* Our doctrine of the judgment has to be something we are proud of, something that makes total sense, that adds grace and richness to the lives of those who accept it, and that will withstand the closest scrutiny (see Romans 1:16; Isaiah 1:18).

What Really Happened in 1844?

ANCHOR POINTS

During the past twenty-plus years, our understanding of the investigative judgment has undergone a great burst of refinement as the church has invested resources in study on this subject. Here are a few of the key anchor points that have received solid support.

1. The judgment is not for God's information and does not take time to complete. An omniscient God is instantly and constantly aware of who belongs to Him (2 Timothy 2:19; John 10:14). So, the traditional concept that during the judgment God discovered who was savable and who was not has been replaced by the idea that the judgment demonstrates to the universe that God is absolutely righteous in the matters of who He saves and how He saves. As Paul wrote: "He did it to demonstrate his justice at the present time, so as to be just and the one who justifies those who have faith in Jesus" (Romans 3:26). And the key verse at the heart of the entire subject, Daniel 8:14, says that at the conclusion of the twenty-three hundred days, the sanctuary will be vindicated, made right.

2. The judgment is not God sitting up in heaven deciding who's in and who's out. As we've discussed earlier, God is a constant, we are the variable. God has already chosen for everyone. He's already done what's necessary to "save" everyone; He died for the sins of the whole world. His love is absolutely constant for every being in the entire universe. He is not willing for any to perish. Jesus pictured the sheep deciding whose voice to follow, rather than the shepherd dividing his flock (see John 10).

The movie *Sophie's Choice* contains a heart-wrenching scene. A mother and her two children, a boy and a girl, are taken into a World War II concentration camp. Children were always separated from their mothers, but in this case a guard took a romantic interest in the woman and offered to spare one of her children—but only one. And she had to choose—"Sophie's choice." One would live and one would die, depending on her choice. Can you imagine making that choice with both of your children looking up at you? The mother couldn't choose. And our God doesn't make that kind of choice. He's chosen all to be saved. He's chosen to give life to all—but each has to choose whether to accept it.

3. The time of the judgment of the living is determined by each individual; it's not an arbitrary time set by God. I grew up, as did many others, with the concept that the judgment in heaven could move into the judgment of the living at any time, and my name could come up and my destiny be sealed. That always bothered me; I wondered how God could settle my destiny when I still had years to live and to make more choices.

I see only two options here. Either God has arbitrarily set the time of the judgment of the living and the time of the close of probation or they are set by cumulative, collective decisions of the human race. One of Satan's lies about God was that He's arbitrary. So I believe the time of the judgment of the living can't be set arbitrarily. The time of the Second Coming is not arbitrary. God knows it, but it is contingent upon the decisions people make. Christ will come when all have made voluntary, free decisions for or against Him.

The same must be true of the close of probation. God won't just say, "I've had it. I'm not waiting any longer for you to get your act together. I'm coming, ready or not!" and close probation. He can't bear to bring everything to closure when there's the slightest chance of saving more people. He waits. He asks, "Is there anything else I can do to convince you, to win your heart? Any other questions I can answer? Any other evidence?" Only when every person has made a personal, voluntary, free, informed decision that God knows and they know is irreversible and irrevocable—only then will God say, "There's nothing more to wait for. I may as well go." Then, and only then, will Jesus utter those famous words: "He that is unjust, let him be unjust still . . . : He that is righteous, let him be righteous still" (Revelation 22:11, KJV).

If all that is true about the Second Coming and the close of probation, then it seems that the same must be true of the judgment of the living. When Ellen G. White wrote that Heaven was about to move from the judgment of the dead to the judgment of the living, it was with a great sense of the imminence of the Second Coming. However, soon after that there began to be references to a delay. And we're now 150 years beyond those references to a delay! Obviously, if each of the other steppingstones toward the Second Coming have been delayed (Sunday laws, etc.), the judgment of the living must have been delayed also. God didn't arbitrarily and irrevocably set some time for it to begin.

People settle their own destiny; they can be judged either when they die and can no longer change their choice or when they become so settled into their beliefs that God knows their decision is unchangeable. People can reach that point at any time, but most will be brought to it collectively near the close of probation, when the latter rain falls and they experience the challenge and excitement of the last days.

4. The judgment of 1844 cannot minimize the Cross and the Second Coming—the great events of salvation history. I want to be very careful, very precise, here. What happened in 1844 is a major part of Adventist history and self-identity. But no matter how significant we consider that event, we must always understand it as "in between" and based upon the two main, critical events of salvation—the Cross/resurrection of Christ and the Second Coming.

The context of much of our understanding of the judgment comes from the book of Daniel, especially the judgment scene of Daniel 7. In Daniel 2:44, the prophet wrote of a stone cut out without hands that will "set up a kingdom that shall never be destroyed." The traditional interpretation has been that this scene points to the Second Coming, when Jesus will set up His eternal kingdom. However, Jesus makes clear that He was already the Stone when He came the first time: "On this rock I will build my church; and the gates of Hades will not overcome it" (Matthew 16:18). Paul and Peter also clearly say that Jesus was already the cornerstone (see Ephesians 2:20; 1 Peter 2:7). And the angel told Mary that her son would "reign over the house of Jacob forever; his kingdom will never end" (Luke 1:33), which appears to be a direct quote from Daniel 2.

It seems clear, then, that the stone in Daniel has two fulfillments: an initial fulfillment at Jesus' first coming, and ultimate fulfillment at His second coming. Jesus established His kingdom when He came the first time; the Stone has been getting larger and larger every time someone joins the kingdom, until someday His kingdom will fill the whole world.

In Daniel 7, there seems to be the same focus on two fulfillments. After the prophet tells about the four empires, he describes this huge courtroom scene in which the Ancient of Days comes to His judgment seat. Then comes the famous verse: "There before me was one like a son of man, coming with the clouds of heaven. He approached the Ancient of Days and was led into his presence" (Daniel 7:13).

When was that fulfilled? Hiram Edson and the early pioneers quickly saw that as a reference to Christ moving into the Most Holy Place in 1844. But notice the context: "He was given authority, glory and sovereign power; all peoples, nations and men of every language worshiped him. His dominion is an everlasting dominion that will not pass away, and his kingdom is one that will never be destroyed" (Daniel 7:14). Clearly, the primary fulfillment is at the Second Coming.

Paralleling this prophecy with that of Daniel 2, however, leads to the conclusion that the initial fulfillment was when Christ entered into the presence of the Father after the Cross and resurrection (see Ephesians 1:20). He ascended to the Father, His sacrifice was accepted and honored, and then the Spirit was poured out at Pentecost. In a sense Christ "received" His kingdom at that time, based upon His sacrifice at the Cross, and He gave the kingdom "proleptically" to the Father. But the ultimate fulfillment will be when Christ hands the church and the kingdom to the Father as His gift at the end of the world.

My barber, Charlie Keyes, told me this story: He went on a cruise. Among his shipmates were a young couple who were on their honeymoon. At one of the ship's stops, the new husband went swimming in the bay, while his bride watched from the steps. He came out of the water heartsick—he had lost his wedding ring. One of the crew came over and asked him where he had been swimming. Then this crew member dived the twenty-five feet to the bottom of the bay over and over again. Finally, he came up and asked, "What does your ring say on it?"

"From Danielle, with love," the man replied.

The crewmember handed it over. What a gift!

That's The Moment—when Christ comes to the Father and hands the kingdom over to Him. It's His gift.

Christ came "to seek and to save what was lost" (Luke 19:10). He said He would come back "and take you to be with me that you also may be where I am" (John 14:3). Take us where? To the Father's house. Into the Father's presence! When will that be completely fulfilled? At the end of the great controversy, when all has been made right, when every question in the judgment has been answered, when everyone and everything is safe, and God has all His friends back again (John 15:15). The little horn is gone, and all the saints are back with God. That's The Moment.

Like Daniel 2 and 7, chapter 8 has its dual fulfillments. The dominant theme in this chapter is the sanctuary and Yom Kippur, the Day of Atonement. The little horn is desolating the sanctuary, but when the sanctuary is finally cleansed, then everything is right again. Yom Kippur.

Clearly the initial fulfillment of Daniel 8 and 9 is at the Cross. The sacrifice of the Lord's goat can only represent the Cross. No one died in our place in 1844 or at the end of the world. When Christ died, He "was sacrificed once to take away the sins of many people" (Hebrews 9:28). He "did away with sin" (Hebrews 9:26). Yom Kippur.

Obviously, however, the antitypical day of atonement is not completely fulfilled until the end of the millennium, when Satan and the demons, symbolized by Azazel, are led out into the wilderness and are no more. Finally, the universe will truly be "at one." "Sin and sinners are no more," as it's put in the famous quote at the end of the book *Great Controversy*.[2] All the dragons and demons and beasts and little horns and Babylons are cast into the lake of fire and gone forever. The entire "camp" is clean. That's Yom Kippur. That's true at-one-ment. That's when the Day of Atonement is fulfilled, and the sanctuary truly has been cleansed. God has all His friends back; everything wrong has been made right. The Shekinah, the glory of God's presence, is everywhere—that is Yom Kippur.

What's the point of all this? Whatever we have to say about 1844 and the judgment must always be said within the context of the two great events of salvation history—the first coming and the second coming of Christ. We can absolutely and legitimately make a solid case for a fulfillment in 1844, but we must first be clear about the two crucial points of salvation: the two comings of Christ.

5. *Judgment is primarily about God.* Many of us grew up thinking the judgment was focused on us. We worried about how we could survive the judgment and make it to heaven and not go to hell. However, the central and primary theme in the Bible is that *God* is the One who is on trial in the judgment, not us! "Fear God, and give him glory, because the hour of *his* judgment is come" (Revelation 14:7). C. S. Lewis wrote an essay called *God in the Dock*. God is the One who's on trial. Rather than Him judging us, we are judging Him. Rather than the records of our actions being reviewed, it is the records of God's actions that must be reviewed. Rather than questions about us being answered, it is questions about God that need to be answered.

Romans contains a key verse. Paul quoted David's prayer of confession to God: " 'So that you may be proved right when you speak and prevail when you judge' " (Romans 3:4). However, it shouldn't have been translated "when you judge," but "when you are judged"! That's how the New American Standard Bible puts it: "THAT THOU MIGHTEST BE JUSTIFIED IN THY WORDS, AND MIGHTEST PREVAIL WHEN THOU ART JUDGED."*

The whole story of Scripture is about the cosmic great controversy between Christ and Satan (Revelation 12; Genesis 3:15). Satan, the father of lies, has insinuated terrible charges against God, challenging His love, fairness, truthfulness, and goodness (see 2 Corinthians 4:4).

Many of us have felt that the judgment has God inside His heavenly fortress while we are outside knocking on the door trying to persuade Him to let us in. No, Scripture says that *we* are on the inside, and God is standing at the door, knocking, trying to persuade

---

*See also: "That thou mayest be justified in thy words, and prevail when thou art judged" (Romans 3:4, RSV); "You must win your case when you are being tried" (TEV); "When thou art on trial" (NEB); "That you may be shown to be upright in what you say, and win your case when you go into court" (Goodspeed).

us that He is good enough for us to let *Him* in (Revelation 3:20). Here's the basic issue in the judgment: Is the Trinity the kind of God we want to have in our lives forever? Do we want to be with this God who is with us everywhere, knows everything about us, and has the power to do anything He wants to us?

A school in Chicago caught fire. A man who lived across the street from the school had a son, Mike, who attended the school. Seeing the fire, the man ran across the street and noticed kids, their faces pressed against the windows, trapped on the second floor. He yelled for them to break a window, and someone did. Then he said, "Now jump!" One by one the boys and girls began to jump, and he caught them. Finally, everyone had jumped except his son. His son froze and then backed away from window. They found his body later. Some people wondered what had happened between father and son that made the son more afraid to jump to his father than to experience the fire.

People wonder about God. That's what the judgment's for—to answer those questions.

This all relates to the central question about the Cross that we wrestled with earlier: Who was the Cross supposed to change? Who was the audience? If God is deciding about us and has questions about us, then He is the One whom the Cross must change. But if we are the ones deciding about Him, pondering questions about Him, then we are the ones the Cross must change. Either the Cross was meant to show God what He needed to see, or it was meant to show us what we need to see. Either the Cross was meant to induce God to love us, or it was meant to induce us to love God.

To summarize, this anchor point says that the judgment is primarily about God. The judgment involves a process just before the end when a group of people (the symbolic 144,000?) who have a white-hot, first-love relationship with God, with "no lie" in their mouths about God, will tell the world what God is really like. The great controversy won't end until everyone has the opportunity to know the true heart of God. Then they'll all make their final decision. In Romans 3, Paul was saying, May You [God] win, may You be victorious, when You are put on trial.

6. *The judgment is against the little horn.* The context of the judgment portrayed in Daniel 7 is clearly the tyranny of the little horn. The little horn comes to power, knocks out three other horns, and speaks "great words against the most High" (Daniel 7:8, 25, KJV). Satan, wanting God's throne, started the war in heaven. If the judgment rules in favor of God, then it must rule against the little horn ("man of sin," "antichrist," "Babylon," "sea beast," etc.). The judgment is not against Christians, against us—it is against the little horn! "The court will sit, and his [the little horn's] power will be taken away and completely destroyed forever" (Daniel 7:26).

The stories of Daniel are illustrations and signs of what will happen to the little horn power. Just as the very Babylonians who threw Daniel's three friends into the fiery furnace ended up there themselves, and just as those who drank from the holy temple vessels ended up "found wanting" and died that very night, and just as those who plotted to overthrow Daniel ended up in the lions' den, so all the Babylonian powers who have spoken against God and persecuted His saints will end up being destroyed.

The message of the judgment is the good news, then, that some day those suffering under the "little horns" of this world will suffer no more. The Babylons and little horns and antichrists of the world will not hold power forever. There will be an end. God will be proven right and the little horn power wrong. All will be made right; justice will prevail. Someday, God will recompense everyone who has ever suffered (see Matthew 19:29; Joel 2:25).

*7. **The judgment is in favor of the saints.*** "The Ancient of Days came and pronounced judgment in favor of the saints of the Most High" (Daniel 7:22). No Christian ever has to fear the judgment. The judgment is good news for all Christians! The judgment is *against* the little horns, but *in favor of* Christians.

Satan has persecuted the saints (Daniel 7:25). He has been the accuser of the brethren (Revelation 12:10). Finally he will be shut up. He will be cast down. The inverse of that means that judgment is in favor of the saints!

Justification is a last-day judgment brought into the present. We are already pronounced justified—righteous and "savable"—the moment we trust in the grace and acceptance of Christ. "God justifies the wicked" (Romans 4:5). " 'Whoever hears my word and believes him who sent me has eternal life and will not be condemned; he has crossed over from death to life' " (John 5:24). Jesus said, " 'I am the gate; whoever enters [the place of safety] through me will be saved' " (John 10:9). The moment we accept Christ, we are justified, and judgment is given in our favor. The charges of the accuser are rejected.

John Ortberg tells a story about a young doctor who got cancer.[3] He went through all the protocols, chemotherapy—the works. When he was tested again, the results that came back indicated that the cancer was back worse than ever. The doctor called Ortberg and cried. He was going to die.

The next morning Ortberg's phone rang again. "I'm not going to die!" the doctor said. "The lab switched the results." He was cancer-free. He couldn't stop hugging his wife and kids. He was going to grow old with them after all.

Unlike the doctor, we actually do have the cancer—sin. The good news of the gospel is that Jesus took our cancer, so now we get His perfect "lab report." We're not going to die; we're going to grow old—very old! And once Jesus trades, He never trades back.

God is a constant. Judgment is in favor of the saints!

In the Bible, judgment is often good news. It is one of the major themes in the Psalms—David begging God to judge his case because he knew the verdict would be in his favor. Daniel 8:14 is actually a longing, a dreaming of the day of judgment, because the sanctuary will finally be made right, be vindicated. The abomination of desolation will be ended forever. Someday there will be Yom Kippur.

Revelation sees Christians as so sealed and settled into their salvation that it actually pictures them as if they were already in heaven. In Revelation 14 and other passages where they are pictured standing on the sea of glass or on Mount Zion, the context makes clear that they are actually still down on this old world! But they are so committed to Christ that, spiritually speaking, they are already standing around God's throne. There is no more condemnation. Judgment has already been given in favor of the saints!

I bought a set of golf clubs, on trial, for thirteen hundred dollars from a telemarketer. When I decided to send them back, I couldn't get through to the company. I had to call my credit card company and put that thirteen-hundred-dollar charge into dispute. Finally, months later, I got my judgment—I didn't owe anything! Judgment is good news for Christians.

8. Christ as judge means Christ is the issue in the judgment. If God is a Constant and has already made His decision to accept everyone into His kingdom, what does it mean when Christ says, " 'The Father judges no one, but has entrusted all judgment to the Son' " (John 5:22)? It means Christ is the *issue* in the judgment. People survive the judgment depending on what they have done about Christ. Remember Pilate's famous question: " 'What shall I do, then, with Jesus who is called Christ?' " (Matthew 27:22).

Lord, I Have a Question

Bill Hybels tells about sailing with friends on San Diego Bay when a huge aircraft carrier entered the bay. All the little sailboats in the regatta had to move to one side or the other; none could stay in the middle. The aircraft carrier didn't decide who went where; it merely made the sailors decide. Similarly, when Christ enters the world, people have to make a decision—left or right? Yes or no? In or out? God is not measuring, evaluating, or establishing a cutoff line and accepting everyone above a certain percentile. He has opened the door to everyone. Christ is the only issue in the judgment.*

"He who has the Son has life; He who does not have the Son does not have life" (1 John 5:12). It can't be much clearer than that! Revelation 1 contains this incredible claim from the resurrected Christ: " 'Do not be afraid. I am the First and the Last. I am the Living One; I was dead, and behold I am alive for ever and ever! And I hold the keys of death and Hades' " (Revelation 1:17, 18). He holds the keys. He *is* the key! And if you have the key, you don't have to be afraid!

My friend Stuart Tyner shared a story with me about a young German who got drafted into Hitler's army during World War II. He was captured and landed in an American POW camp. An American soldier made friends with him. One day, all the prisoners were being formed into lines, when all of a sudden his friend grabbed him by the shoulder, jerked him out of one line and into the another, and motioned for him to be silent. He found out later that the first line he'd been in had been marched to the Russian allies, where all of them were shot. Eventually, this prisoner was shipped to a POW camp in the States. He ended up staying here, became an Adventist, worked for the Review and Herald Publishing Association most of his life, and died only a few years ago! His whole life depended on being in the right line, and he was in the right line

---

*See Luke 2:34; John 3:18.

because he was a friend of the right person! "He who has the Son has life."

H. M. S. Richards, Sr., used to say, "I have only one doctrine: I am a great sinner—but I have a great Savior." During an interview once at Pacific Union College he was asked, "What is the Adventist message?" He replied, "Jesus only." There's a famous story about the great theologian Dr. Karl Barth. A seminary student asked him, "If you had to boil everything you've written, all you've studied, all of Christianity, down to one idea, what would it be?" Barth said, "Jesus loves me, this I know, for the Bible tells me so."

The ultimate issue in the judgment is whether we have accepted the picture of God presented in Jesus:

> The enemy of good blinded the minds of men, so that they looked upon God with fear; they thought of Him as severe and unforgiving, . . . watching with jealous eye to discern the errors and mistakes of men, that He may visit judgments upon them. It was to remove this dark shadow, by revealing to the world the infinite love of God, that Jesus came to live among men.[4]

9. The key to the judgment is grace. Many people have been terrified that God starts us off with grace, but when we get to the judgment, we're going to have to be perfect all on our own. They have heard about living without a mediator.* But God never uses "bait and switch." He never starts with grace and then ends up demanding

---

*One of the perennial questions people ask pastors is, Why does it seem so hard? They've read the "narrow" texts in the Bible (e.g., Matthew 7:13; 19:25; 22:14; Luke 13:23) and have concluded that it is almost impossible to survive the judgment. We must balance those texts with all the "wide" texts: (Matthew 19:26; John 3:16; 10:7, 9; 2 Peter 3:9; Revelation 3:8). John saw "a great multitude, that no man can number" (Revelation 7:9). If they could count 200 million demons (Revelation 9:16; symbolic, no doubt), but no one could count the multitude who are saved, then the door to salvation is very wide! Everybody who wants in can enter.

perfection. Yes, God calls us to live victorious, godly lives, but that will never become the basis on which we make it through the judgment. It is first, middle, last, and always Christ and grace. "Jesus Christ is the same yesterday and today and forever" (Hebrews 13:8). "I consider everything a loss compared to the surpassing greatness of knowing Christ Jesus my Lord . . . that I may gain Christ and be found in him" (Philippians 3:8, 9).*

10. The judgment is a serious time. People have wondered, If we admit that the fulfillment of the Day of Atonement began at the Cross and continues until sin is eradicated from the entire universe, what role is left to 1844? While I'll say more about this later, a central theme is certainly that the judgment is a serious time. This is *not* cheap grace. Our works are involved: First, our works show that our faith is serious. Our works are *never* the basis of passing the judgment, but everyone saved by grace is empowered by the Spirit to live God-honoring lives. And second, our works help complete the judgment by bringing glory to God, drawing people to God, showing the world what God is truly like. Our works show people the character of God in real, concrete terms. So, our works help God win His "trial" and help bring the judgment to a conclusion.†

God clearly means for the judgment to be a serious time, when we take ultimate choices very seriously. The fact that God bases our salvation on grace doesn't mean we can take on a cavalier attitude.

Two men from the gas company were out checking meters. At the end of the street the supervisor challenged the younger man to a race back to their truck. When they reached the truck, the lady from

---

*See also Galatians 3:3; Philippians 1:6; Revelation 14:6. White, *Review and Herald,* April 1, 1890.

†"The honor of God, the honor of Christ, is involved in the perfection of the character of His people" (White, *Desire of Ages,* 671).

the last house they checked was running right behind them, huffing and puffing. "What's wrong?" they asked.

She said, "When I see two guys from the gas company running like crazy, I figure I'M OUTTA HERE!!"

When God starts talking about judgment and the last days, take it seriously! No one's going to be able to run away from the judgment. While God's on trial, it's going to include all of us. Everyone will have seen all the evidence in the final showdown between good and evil, and will have made their final, eternal choice, with life-or-death consequences. It is very serious!

STAGES OF THE JUDGMENT

The judgment happens in stages:

1. Christ's death. The moment Christ cried, "It is finished!" and died was the moment of complete atonement for us, the announcement that all our sins were forgiven. Jesus said, "Now is the time for judgment on this world" (John 12:31).

2. Justification. The moment anyone accepts Christ or chooses not to reject His grace, that moment is the judgment of justification (John 5:24).

3. The year 1844—judgment time began. For two thousand years God has wanted to bring everything to a head. In 1844, He had everything lined up—the last days, the dark day, the falling of the stars, the call to Ellen White, William Miller, a renewed focus on Christ as high priest, the truth about God, the seventh-day Sabbath in the ark in the Most Holy Place, and the three angels' messages being preached.

God started a community of people to give His last-day message to the world—a message telling what He's really like, an open door right into the heart of God in the Most Holy Place in heaven. He wanted a people to clarify to the world the relationship between His grace and His law in the Ark of the Covenant. God wants the entire universe to know that those He saves, He saves legitimately, so that no one could question His goodness and fairness. And He gave the enemy every chance to make his case.

Unfortunately, there's been a delay. But when everything's lined up again, the final countdown will go in a hurry.

4. *Close of probation.* By the close of probation, everyone has made their own sealed and settled decision, and therefore they've settled their own judgment. All those throughout the universe who have been watching can see that God has demonstrated His justice in giving life to those who have chosen Him (Romans 3:25, 26).

5. *Second Coming and the millennium.* God allows the saints to spend a thousand years in peace and safety in heaven, building community, healing from the trauma of this world, and going over the books—"judging" (Revelation 20:1-6). God wants every question answered once and for all, in case any might wonder if God could have done more, or why certain loved ones are not in heaven. The new earth will be safe and free only if every question has been answered, so that "trouble will not come a second time" (Nahum 1:9).

During Bill Clinton's campaign for the presidency in 1992, scandal after scandal surfaced, raising questions about character. Clinton always chose to use some euphemism or verbal sleight-of-hand to try to minimize full accountability for his actions. His campaign struggled because of the constant effort to avoid being destroyed by these allegations. Later, we heard that Clinton's aides begged him to call a press conference and answer every question absolutely truthfully and fully until every reporter was totally satisfied and thus to put these questions behind them once and for all. Clinton refused to do it and has had to live with the questions and their consequences to this day.[5] God doesn't want that. He wants to end the questions forever—so, a judgment.

6. Great white throne judgment. Revelation 20:11 points to a final, postmillennial judgment, after all the wicked have been raised. When they see the New Jerusalem, they attack it, showing that even after a thousand years of mulling everything over, nothing has changed for Satan and the demons. The great white throne judgment will in some way portray the entire great controversy saga. At its conclusion, "at the name of Jesus every knee should bow . . . and every tongue confess that Jesus Christ is Lord, to the glory of God the Father" (Philippians 2:10, 11).

All will say with Daniel, "The LORD OUR GOD is righteous in everything he does" (Daniel 9:14). Those who have watched the conflict for so long will all praise God for His fairness, His justice (Revelation 5:13; 15:3, 4; 16:5, 7; 19:2). When the wicked finally die, they will all die having freely acknowledged that God did everything exactly right in every way. What a witness that will be for all the righteous and all the unfallen beings in the universe! No one will ever again wonder whether the wicked have been treated fairly—the wicked *themselves* will have acknowledged that what happens at the end is absolutely righteous. The universe can be forever at-one.

One final picture of the judgment: John Grisham is a Christian who writes stories set in the legal system. In *The Firm*, he pictured a young attorney who is working sixty to seventy hours a week while also studying for the bar exam. He finds out his firm is working for the Mafia and starts to steal evidence. His house is bugged; his phone is bugged. He knows he could be caught any time.

He walks into the law offices one day, and someone grabs him and says, "The boss wants to see you." He takes him by the arm into the elevator and up to the top floor. The young attorney is sure they've caught him, that it's all over. He walks through the door into this huge office, and every lawyer in the firm is there. Even his wife is there. Then the senior partner says, "Congratulations—you passed the bar! You didn't get first place . . . but you did get second . . . in the entire nation!" And they all cheer and slap him on the back.

That's how the judgment is going to be for us. Now we're afraid, terrified of that moment when an angel will take us by the arm and lead us up to the top floor. We know that they've been listening to every word we've ever said. They have pictures of everything we've ever done! And they're all going to be there: God the Father, God the Son, God the Holy Spirit, and ten thousand times ten thousand holy angels. When they start reading, though, there won't be any sins on the records! They're all gone, destroyed, shredded. But there will be every dollar, every act of service, every gift we've given, every hour in some ministry.

I believe there will be moments when Christ, with tears streaming down His face, will stop the reading and say, "When you did it for them, you did it for Me. You'll never know what that meant to us that day! People were yelling and screaming at us all around the world—and then you did that. You'll never know what that meant to us!"

That's what the judgment will really be like if you're in Christ!

---

1. White, *Great Controversy*, 483.

2. Ibid., 678.

3. John Ortberg, *The Life You've Always Wanted: Spiritual Disciplines for Ordinary People* (Grand Rapids, Mich.: Zondervan, 1997), 69, 70.

4. White, *Steps to Christ*, 10, 11.

5. See *Time*, Special Election issue, (November 2, 1992) vol. 140, no. 20.

CHAPTER NINE

The Problem of Evil and Suffering

"Where is God?"

Elie Wiesel, the Nobel Prize winner, was a young Jew in a concentration camp during World War II. One morning the inmates were forced to stand in the snow while the Germans hung three Jews—two men and a young boy. The men were heavy and so died quickly. But the boy was light, so he hung there choking for half an hour before dying. Wiesel remembers that during the half-hour the inmates were forced to watch, one of them screamed out, "Where is God?" Wiesel has spent the rest of his life working out answers to that question.[1]

Millions throughout history have asked that question. It's a question that may be even harder to answer than those questions regarding God's existence. Very few people in the world are hard-core atheists, but nearly everyone struggles with questions like, Why does God allow so much suffering? Why do good people have to suffer from chronic pain, liver cancer, and quadriplegia? Why are innocent little girls sexually abused? Why aren't there more of the biblical miracles today? If we had more faith or prayed harder or had more people pray, would we get more answers to prayer? Why pray, if God already knows everything and has all the power in the world?

We have to be honest with the evidence. As I write this, fires are raging all over southern California. Houses for which people have prayed have been destroyed. Millions of Christians have prayed for protection, yet have died. Millions of Christians have prayed for healing, yet have remained sick or died. And millions have begged God for financial help but are still poor.

Fred Craddock tells a story about a young pastor who goes to the hospital to visit with an old woman who's dying, gasping for breath. Eventually the pastor says, "I have to go, would you like me to pray?"

"Yes."

"What would you like me to pray for?"

"That I'd be healed, of course."

The preacher gulps, prays a halting prayer for her to be healed, but if not, that God would give her the grace to adjust to her circumstances. Suddenly the old woman opens her eyes, sits up, throws her feet over the side of the bed, and stands up, saying, "I think I'm healed!" She strides out the door of the room, yelling at the nurses, "Look at me!"

The pastor goes out to the parking lot, and before he gets into his car, he looks up and says, "Don't You *ever* do that to me again!"

Why would he ask that? Maybe so he would not begin to build up hope for more spectacular miracles, only to have his hopes dashed. We have to be honest and look at the flip side of every miracle—why that miracle and not others? Why did some get out of the Twin Towers on September 11, while others didn't? Every time a soldier comes home safe and everyone claims it as an answer to prayer, we have to ask, "What about those who were prayed for who didn't come home?" C. S. Lewis wrote: "Every war, every famine or plague, almost every death-bed, is the monument to a petition that was not granted."[2]

He also asked our question:

> Meanwhile, where is God? . . . When you are happy . . . [and] have no sense of needing Him . . . you will be . . . welcomed with open arms. But go to Him when your need is desperate, when all other help is vain, and what do you find?

The Problem of Evil and Suffering

A door slammed in your face, and a sound of bolting and double bolting on the inside. After that, silence. You may as well turn away. The longer you wait, the more emphatic the silence will become. There are no lights in the windows.[3]

And what about the "half miracles"? There's a car accident, and the passengers survive—thanking God for the miracle, but they're injured. My cynical mind can't help asking that if God used His power to intervene, why He didn't use enough power to keep the accident from happening in the first place? And how come God can see fit to send fifty dollars to a missionary in Costa Rica, but somehow not to heal the spine of Joni Eareckson Tada? Why does He solve only the trivial when He has the power to speak entire universes into existence?

The subject is often called *theodicy*, "justifying God." Obviously, if we are going to wrestle with the character of God, we are going to have to deal with this set of questions before we're done. How can we reconcile the picture of God as a God of love and goodness with this Person who has the power to relieve every bit of suffering people are experiencing and chooses to keep that power in His pocket? We would step in; why doesn't God?

Obviously, in two chapters in a book we are not going to cover the entire subject. But if we're dealing with the character of God, there is no way we can really avoid this cluster of issues, so let's have a go, beginning with a review of some of our nonnegotiable anchor points. Whatever theology of suffering, prayer, and miracles we come up with, it cannot compromise the following anchor points.

NONNEGOTIABLE ANCHOR POINTS
*1. God is infinitely and perfectly good and loving all the time.** Under no circumstance does God ever will the existence of evil. He cannot get any better than He already is. Our prayers will never in-

---

*1 John 4:8, 16; Psalm 34:8; Malachi 3:6; Hebrews 13:8.

crease His goodness or His desire to do good for His people. He wants the very best for everyone.* He gives His sunshine and rain to the "just and the unjust." He pours out life, grace, love, and acceptance to all equally—He loves even His enemies.

2. *God is righteous in everything He does.*[†] When we have a chance to "review the books" and see the end from the beginning, we will never—not one single time—feel that we would have handled it differently than God has. We will never say, "I think maybe You blew this one, God; You should have stepped in!"

3. *God gives only life; everything He does supports life.*[‡]

4. *God is all three omni's: omnipotent, omniscient, and omnipresent.* There is nothing that is logically possible that He can't do. This means that we can't answer the question about evil's existence by saying that God is not powerful enough to counteract that evil, as Rabbi Kushner suggested in his book *When Bad Things Happen to Good People.* There is nothing knowable that God doesn't know. And there is no place where God can't project His power.

5. *God the Father is just as anxious to bless as is Christ.*[§] That Christ is our intercessor doesn't mean that we must use Christ to persuade the Father to bless us. Christ is our window to the truth about God, and He showed that They are exactly the same in character. God is One.

6. *Satan is the source of evil, pain, and suffering.*[**]

7. *God is absolutely committed to respecting free choice.*[††]

8. *God is always working.*[‡‡] And He is always working to the ultimate. He'll never be vulnerable to the criticism or challenge that He worked harder at some times than at others or worked harder for some people than for others or used more heavenly resources for some people than for others.

---

*Matthew 5:43-48; 3 John 2; Jeremiah. 29:11; Luke 11:13.

†Daniel 9:14; Revelation 15:3, 4; 19:2.

‡John 10:10; 6:63.

§John 14:6, 9; 1:18; 10:30; 16:26, 27; Hebrews 1:1-3.

**Matthew 13:28.

††Joshua 24:15; Hebrews 2:3; Luke 15; Matthew 23:37, 38.

‡‡John 5:17.

The Problem of Evil and Suffering

To be intellectually honest, we have to include observations of the evidence that we see in the development of our theology of suffering and miracles. If we read a text that sounds like we can receive from God whatever we ask for in prayer in Jesus' name and then observe a thousand people pray for a particular thing without "success," we may have to go back to the text and see if perhaps the rest of Scripture contains limitations, caveats, and fine print that might help us match our expectations with the reality we experience. Scripture *always* has the last word, but we cannot maintain any kind of credibility if we blithely ignore massive amounts of evidence that seems to contradict our understanding of the Bible.

I've been a pastor a long time, and I have talked to many, many other pastors to see if their experience was any better than mine. When we have an anointing prayer, we have terrific prayer times, and God seems very close and gracious. But far too many times, we still have a funeral in the next few weeks or months.

As a young pastor, I was once asked to drive up from southern Oregon to Walla Walla College to resurrect a young man who had just been killed by a terrible head-on collision with a truck. I wasn't sure what we would do—what if it worked! Would we hug him? What would it be like to spend nine hours in a car with a man who had just been dead?

How many people are you aware of who have been raised from the dead? Not many! How many quadriplegics have been cured? Paraplegics? How many people have been cured—not just had temporary remissions—of a terminal cancer like liver cancer? Not many. How many people have been cured of more minor problems? We know of a few more stories like that. How many people have received money that seemed to be a miracle or an answer to prayer? There are thousands of stories like that. And how many people have been spiritually and morally changed and experienced the change the day they accepted Christ? There are millions of stories like that. If our collective experience is representative at all, maybe this chart is pretty close to reality:

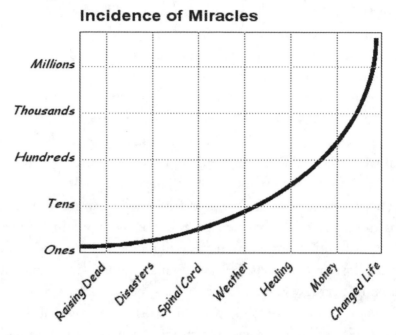

Inductive logic and observation of modern-day miracles leads to the conclusion that today, God's work seems to be primarily internal rather than external, spiritual rather than physical.

What does the trend indicate? Doesn't it clearly indicate that, as God works within the limits of the great controversy, we have no right to expect that He will reverse all evil in our world before the second comming, no matter how much faith we have or how many prayers we offer or how holy the individuals praying might be? It seems clear that God's work is more internal than external, more spiritual than physical. And the miracles that are the most prevalent are those that occur when God impresses one person to help another.

So, we must develop a theology of evil and suffering that includes the inspired evidence we read in Scripture and the Spirit of Prophecy, but that also matches the reality we experience on the street.

The Problem of Evil and Suffering

GUIDELINES FOR A THEOLOGY OF EVIL AND SUFFERING

1. All evil and suffering come from Satan, not from God. Insurance companies call disasters "acts of God." I have a thick file of statements by people who have experienced terrible disasters or disappointments and attributed them to God's will—for example, Magic Johnson getting HIV, Jackie Robinson's health problems, Dan Janssen falling in the Olympics, David Allison's helicopter crash, and many others. When Jesus said, "An enemy did this" (Matthew 13:28), He was talking specifically about evil people in the church. But we demean God when we blame Him for *any* evil. Jesus said that He is not a thief—"I came to give life!" (see John 10:10).

2. God is absolutely committed to free choice. God created people in His image, which means He gave them volition, free choice. He will never overrule our free choice. If He were to bless only Christians, that would unduly force unbelievers to believe out of sheer self-interest. If God intervenes too obviously in the real, physical world, then unbelievers cannot choose to disbelieve and retain their sanity. And so God has to allow evildoers the freedom to do what their nature dictates. A universe of love has to be a universe of free choice. Love without choice is not love.

In 2002, my father died in a tragic hit-and-run accident. He was walking near his home when a man in a small truck drove up onto the sidewalk and hit him. He died that night in the ICU, with all his family around him. He never regained consciousness. He was a wonderful man, a pastor, a missionary.

Now, the family I grew up in has a strong Christian—Adventist—history. But suppose a Buddhist monk had walked into Dad's hospital room right after he died, laid his hands on him, uttered some incantations, and all of a sudden the heart monitor registered a heartbeat, Dad began to breathe again and opened his eyes and began to talk to us, and then he got up and walked out the door with us. My brothers and I would all have been Buddhists in the morning! That's the kind of coercive power God has to be very careful about exercising. That's why He often has to work "in the shadows" and allow the appearance of naturalistic explanations for even those times when He does supernaturally intervene.

A corollary to this is that *God wants no "rice Christians."* He wants no one to come to Him only for material, personal gain. He wants a relationship, a friendship (Revelation 3:20; John 15:15). He wants to be loved for who He is. So He has to find a careful balance between doing enough to draw us to Him and to satisfy basic needs without offering so much that people's choices and motives become skewed. At times He may even have to withdraw the material, physical confirmations of His presence to purify our faith, so that we will trust Him regardless of the "blessings" He may bestow.*

3. To win the great controversy, God has to give Satan a fairly level playing field. He has to give him an equitable opportunity to demonstrate the truthfulness of his charges about God and of his claim that people who follow him instead of God will become like gods. God has to honor the free choice of Satan and the demons. He can't afford to give Satan or any other being an excuse to question whether the alternative to God might have been better.†

4. God has to preserve a certain predictability in the universe. For God's universe to be permanently safe, every being will have learned to understand and accept the laws of reality—cause and effect. God doesn't want to keep heaven safe by force or power or threats. He wants the natural consequences of evil and righteousness to be so clear that there's no risk of evil arising again.

---

*See Habakkuk's wonderful testimony in Habakkuk 3:17, 18.
†Job 1; Nahum 1:9.

5. The plan of salvation contains a "not yet." We can't pray our way to a heaven on earth today. "Thy will be done on earth as it is in heaven" is a prayer we will pray until we enter the kingdom. If it were to be answered fully today, Jesus wouldn't need to go to prepare a place for us; we would already have heaven here!

God has chosen to come in two stages. Christ inaugurated the last days, but they will not be consummated until the Second Coming and the new earth. We live "between the times," in two worlds, in two kingdoms.* We live in the time of the "not yet" (Hebrews 11:35-40). We cannot pray our way to creating a heaven down here now. That is for the future. That is "not yet." Only when the New Jerusalem comes down out of heaven will there be "no more tears, no more pain, no more death."

6. Dominion will be fully restored in the new earth. God gave Adam and Eve dominion over the Garden of Eden, to care for it. They lost that dominion at the Fall and came under the "curse" of the natural consequences of sin (Genesis 3:15). During his farewell sermon, Moses described the incredible blessings the Israelites would enjoy if they obeyed all God's commands—they would be the head and not the tail, etc. (see Deuteronomy 28-30). But he also described the "curses" that would come if they disobeyed. Obviously, they disobeyed! They sinned, they ended up in captivity, and many rejected Christ as the Messiah and refused their role as God's witnesses to the world.

However—and it's a huge however!—"Christ redeemed us from the curse of the law by becoming a curse for us. . . . He redeemed us in order that the blessing given to Abraham might come to the Gentiles through Christ Jesus, so that by faith we might receive the promise of the Spirit" (Galatians 3:13, 14).

---

*Galatians 1:3, 4; Hebrews 6:4-6; 11; John 18:36; Mark 1:14, 15; Luke 17:20, 21.

When Jesus read the messianic prophecy from Isaiah 61, He applied it to Himself: " 'The Spirit of the Lord is on me, because he has anointed me to preach good news to the poor. He has sent me to proclaim freedom for the prisoners and recovery of sight for the blind, to release the oppressed, to proclaim the year of the Lord's favor. . . . Today this scripture is fulfilled in your hearing' " (Luke 4:18-21).

Jesus died to redeem us from the curse, so that instead of having to live under all the consequences of sin, we can begin to live under the rich blessings of the Spirit. The restoration of dominion has begun. The reality of the new kingdom has come; we live under the new covenant. We begin today to experience the "powers of the coming age" (Hebrews 6:4, 5).

Because of this fact, several TV preachers and others have suggested that we should *now* live free from *all* the consequences of evil. I have often had members quote to me the biblical line, "By His wounds we are healed" (Isaiah 53:5; 1 Peter 2:24). Then they demand, "If Christ has redeemed us from the curse, and we are healed by His wounds, why can't we expect that God will heal all diseases and protect us from every disaster and every other consequence of sin and evil?"

The answer lies in the fact of the "not yet" in which we live. We have *some* of the realities of the future kingdom, but not *all* of them. Sin no longer *reigns*, but it still *remains*. We still have sin in our lives; we are in the process of being sanctified, but sin is not completely gone. *If Christ's redemption of sin in our lives is a lifelong process completed only when we go to heaven, then, by extension, we can assume that the results of sin will not be fully redeemed until we pass through the gates of heaven.*

7. Until we have learned the consequences of sin, God has chosen to limit His use of His omnipotent power to preserve freedom of choice. This is the huge difference between the great controversy explanation of evil and suffering and that of Rabbi Kushner. We believe that God has all power and that He uses all of it constantly for good *except* when it would conflict with the goals of the great controversy. It is clear in Revelation 7 that God has the angels of heaven holding back the winds of strife. In His ultimate wisdom and knowledge, seeing the end from the beginning, God has determined that the line between good and evil that He has chosen is *exactly* the correct line. He is balancing, on the one hand, using His power to limit evil, and on the other, allowing free choice to determine a great deal of the reality we experience.

God has chosen to allow some suffering today so that in the future, heaven will be free from suffering. The community who live there will have learned all about the consequences of sin and living apart from God, ensuring that it can be safe forever. He considers the party that we'll enjoy then worth the agony of not stepping in to eradicate all suffering today.

As we will see in Chapter 11, in the last days God will have to cut back the use of His power even further in order to demonstrate unequivocally what life would be like in a world without God, in a kingdom dominated by Satan. That final showdown will help settle the questions of evil and of God's goodness once and for all for every being in the universe, and each being will make an eternal choice.

8. We can never "break the code" on God. His methods are far beyond our ability to penetrate. He is always "outside the box." Often we can see His absence better than His presence. He is not a heavenly jukebox, as some have joked, into which you put your quarters or your prayers or whatever the formula is, and out come miracles and answers to prayer and absolute protection and elimination of evil. He isn't the cosmic genie, guaranteeing to fulfill all of our deepest desires and wishes here and now.

But in Scripture and in the broad trends of how and where God seems to be working in the world, we may be able to discern some patterns that can reveal to some degree how God works in the great controversy.

9. There is a great distinction between what God does externally and internally. Years ago I read a very interesting article in *Christianity Today* by Paul Brand and Philip Yancey.[4] In that article, Brand, a Christian surgeon who worked for many years with lepers in India, wrote that in all his experience he had noticed that nearly all miracles or healings he had observed had been of one particular type, and few or none of any other type. Why would God arbitrarily discriminate regarding the situations in which He chose to intervene? The authors suggested that God is obviously choosing to operate in cooperation with certain faculties He placed within human beings. The vast majority of the healings involved those diseases susceptible to healing by a partnership between God's power and those human healing faculties.

Since then I have thought a lot about that. My thoughts led to the chart on page 132, which illustrates that God tends to work *internally* rather than *externally*. Where people's prayer has given Him freedom to work within someone's mind (impressions to swerve to avoid a truck, for example), miracles can happen. But it seems He rarely moves sheet metal around.

And He works primarily *spiritually* rather than *physically*. With problems amenable to a doctor's care, we have miracles. With problems such as inadequate finances or food or shelter or transportation—problems that some other person with resources can solve—there are miracles. But God doesn't seem to choose to restore severed nerves in spinal columns.

Matthew 5 should have pointed us in that direction all along. God sends His sun and rain on all. *God's blessings are indiscriminate externally, but discriminate internally.* God pours out certain kinds of blessing on everyone: life, grace, love, forgiveness. His grace is indiscriminate; He makes no distinctions. He is working through the Holy

Spirit to win everyone to Him. He is whispering life-giving counsel to everyone. However, to continue the metaphor, though God sends the sun equally all around the world, people can choose to stay in the dark. They can reject God's grace. They can tune out His life-giving counsel. God's grace can work greater miracles internally within Christians, because through faith and prayer they have allowed Him greater access to their lives.

So, God doesn't automatically keep Christians healthier, protect them more, or make their stocks increase in value faster than other stocks. On external matters, He blesses all equally. The benefit in being a Christian comes internally. We can choose to be more open to His grace, to His love, to His Spirit and power. We can learn to tune in to His counsel. We can read and meditate on His revelation. We can bask in His spiritual presence.

10. God has chosen to "allow" suffering only in the generic, not the specific, sense. His limiting of suffering (Job 1; Revelation 7:1-4) simply means that He has restricted Satan to causing a certain range of evil, pain, and suffering. In general, it does not mean that God picks the winners and losers.* It does not mean that God looks down from heaven and says, "That little girl can be molested, and that little girl, but not this one. He can have cancer, but not her. These people can go down with the plane, but not those people." How can we answer the people who were stretched on the rack in the Tower of London or massacred in Rwanda or gassed or experimented on during the Holocaust as to why God chose to allow them to suffer these unspeakable horrors?

---

*Job seems to be most glaring exception. God may have had good reasons for allowing the great controversy issues to be played out in a microcosm in Job's case to highlight all the issues. But it would be dangerous to generalize from his case to all cases and presume that *in every single case* of suffering God made a specific choice, after weighing all the circumstances, possible benefits, and negative consequences, and chose to allow specific people to suffer such unspeakable horrors as sexual abuse, chronic pain, or Nazi medical experimentation.

The text most often quoted in support of the "allowing" motif is: "No temptation has seized you except what is common to man. And God is faithful, he will not let you be tempted beyond what you can bear. But when you are tempted, he will also provide a way out so that you can stand up under it" (1 Corinthians 10:13). People interpret that to mean that God has specifically allowed some sort of suffering to teach certain people vital spiritual lessons. Or because He knew they could handle it the best. Or He allows some to die in order to wake others up spiritually. Or because He knew that they were ready to go and if He allowed them to live, they would later apostatize and be lost (which means that all of us still alive are not safe yet to be "harvested"!).

This text isn't primarily about suffering. It is referring to *temptation!* God allows no temptation to come to us that He is not able to give us power to escape. His grace and the power of the Holy Spirit can give us victory over all temptation (Jude 24)! People have endured unbelievable torture that was certainly beyond their capacity to endure. You can't tell me that God in heaven weighed everything and made the specific, personalized decision to directly allow that torture.

Years ago, I decided that many examples of suffering had no "silver lining." For instance, I could think of virtually no good that resulted from the death of Jews in the Holocaust or in the pogroms of Russia. Or the millions killed under Stalin. Or the one-third of all little girls reportedly damaged by some form of abuse. Nothing makes these atrocities "worth it." When planes go down or hurricanes or earthquakes destroy thousands, I can't believe that God determined that some greater benefit was served by their dying than by their continuing to live.

People search for meaning and purpose in their suffering, I know. But ultimately the answer is that we live in a broken world where evil is often random; there is no pattern. Yes, God can often redeem the evil and bring some good out of it. But that is virtually never the reason for allowing specific instances of evil. Only in the universal sense is there any redeeming value and purpose; God knows He must allow evil in order for all of us to learn once and for all the terrible connection between sin and disaster, between leaving the Father's home and ending up alone, destitute, and hungry in the pigsty in the "far country."

My father didn't die because his life hadn't been holy and righteous enough. He didn't die because my mother and my brothers and I didn't have enough faith. He didn't die because we had some spiritual lesson to learn or to wake up a group of people, to jolt them into being more spiritually alive. He lived in a broken world where people lose control of cars or go crazy for a moment or lose their judgment because of drugs. Someday, we will live in a world where all of this will be made right. But not now. Not yet.

Yes, I hope with all my heart that my father's death makes us all more serious about our relationships with God and with our loved ones, and that we will follow the example of his humble life of service: caring about people, giving Bible studies, going out of the way to visit people in prison, and running errands for shut-ins. But my brothers and I don't believe for a second that God weighed any of that in "allowing" our father to die. God is not that kind of God. In the meantime, "we have this hope" that someday we will go from the "not yet" to the "now!"

---

1. Elie Wiesel, *Night, Dawn, Day,* Stelle Rodway, trans. (Northvale, N.J.: Aronson, 1985), 71.

2. C. S. Lewis, *Letters to Malcolm: Chiefly on Prayer* (San Diego: Harcourt Brace Jovanovich, 1963), 58.

3. Lewis, *A Grief Observed* (New York: Bantam Books, 1961), 4, 5.

4. Paul Brand and Philip Yancey, "A Surgeon's View of Divine Healing," *Christianity Today*, November 25, 1983 (available at <www.christianitytoday.com>).

CHAPTER TEN

What About Miracles and Prayer?

Why don't we see more miracles today? Did they cease at the end of the first century? Does prayer do any good? Does it change God? Why pray if God already knows everything? Why pray if God is already doing His best? Why pray for others if God won't change their minds against their will? Would God answer more of our prayers if we had more faith?

We've already said much that has prepared us to deal with the question of why we don't see more miracles today. As we focus more closely on prayer and miracles, I should state clearly that I believe in miracles. I don't accept *cessationism,* which is the belief that miracles and other signs of the Spirit ceased after the age of Christ and the apostles, after the biblical canon was closed. I celebrate every miracle that happens. I accept Paul's counsel to the Thessalonians to avoid quenching the Spirit, but to test everything that claims to be miraculous (see 1 Thessalonians 5:19-22).

What are the key points of a view of miracles that fits the biblical passages that seem to promise anything we ask yet also fits the practical evidence of hospitals filled with acutely sick patients, billions of poor people, and cemeteries full of funerals, flowers, and gravestones?

What About Miracles and Prayer?

MIRACLES

1. The miracles recorded in Scripture aren't evenly distributed throughout the time span it covers. It seems clear that the miracles of the Bible are generally clustered around the great moments of religious history—the times of the Exodus, of Elijah and Elisha, and of Christ and the early church and apostles. Spreading these recorded miracles throughout the fifteen hundred years of biblical history reveals that they were really quite rare. We should be cautious, then, about extrapolating from the Bible that we should expect to be experiencing miracles every day. The fact that they were clustered around these great events in salvation history and were not everyday experiences should also tell us something about how and why God uses miracles.

Building upon the previous chapter, we can add the following points:

2. The physical miracles were signs of what God wants to do for us spiritually; they are not promises of what we can expect physically every day. The crossing of the Red Sea was a sign of our spiritual crossing over to the Promised Land, when we will triumph over the enemies of God and live in peace forever. The feeding of the five thousand was a sign that Christ wants to be our spiritual Bread of Life. Christ healed the man born blind as a sign that He is the Light of the world, the clearest picture of God. His calming the storm was a sign that He offers us inner, spiritual peace. In many cases, the Gospel writers put the miracle in the same context as the sermon that the miracle illustrated (see, for example, John 6).

3. God uses unnatural means to teach the natural, intrinsic benefits of a relationship with Him and of living a godly, moral life. In other words, God wants us to know that He can heal every kind of spiritual and emotional damage that we have accumulated. He uses the *physical* healing miracles in hope that we will learn the *spiritual* lesson that we need to be healed by Him. (The Greek word translated "salvation" actually means "healing.") God hopes we will learn that living by His healing grace and the therapeutic guidelines in the commandments and elsewhere in Scripture will enhance the quality of our lives. Remember, He's the One who says, "I am not a thief; I came to give life. My words are life!"

For example, He uses the feeding of the five thousand, the very unnatural miracle of multiplying food, to illustrate the benefits of "eating" His words, His teaching. Scripture says that those who ate the food Jesus provided were filled, satisfied. We can have the same sense of being filled, of being spiritually satisfied, only by "consuming" Jesus' teaching. We get into trouble when we miss the link and assume that Jesus meant for us to ask Him to repeat all the biblical miracles physically, over and over again. That was never the point.

4. The physical miracles will be repeated physically during the millennium. While the miracles were not signs of what God will do physically for us now, they were signs of what God is planning to do physically at the final consummation, in the eternal kingdom. We won't walk on water until we walk on the sea of glass. We won't cross over completely into the Promised Land until we enter the kingdom. We won't experience total physical healing until sin has been banished from the universe forever.

5. The miracles done individually by Christ, the apostles, and the prophets are fulfilled today primarily by the collective Body of Christ. Yes, once in a while someone may experience a miracle of healing today. But God has designed a health message and a healthcare mission that have contributed to the healing of millions around the world. The healings effected by healthcare specialists and as the result of scientific research may be the result of impressions from God. They may be as miraculous as the healings Christ did by placing His hands on people and putting mud on their eyes!

God fed five thousand men plus women and children by multiplying a few fish and loaves of bread. Now He feeds the hungry through the body of Christ. Just as He used what one little boy gave and then distributed it through the disciples, so He now feeds millions through blessing what generous people give and then using His modern-day disciples to distribute it to the world.

Christ cast demons out of individuals by speaking. He has given the church the power and responsibility to cast evil out of the world—to release people from demon possession and turn them into sane, God-honoring disciples—through preaching, counseling, education, and prayer ministry. Today, rather than simply intervening Himself, God often uses people as the answer to prayers. This is at least a major meaning of Jesus' statement that "He that believeth on me, the works that I do shall he do also; and greater works than these shall he do; because I go unto my Father" (John 14:12, KJV). Jesus' miracles were limited by space and time. The miracles God does now through the body of Christ can happen constantly and simultaneously all around the world.

So, can we still pray for miracles? Yes, as we will see in what follows. Are miracles still happening today? Yes; we do not believe in cessationism. Should we expect miracles every day and blame ourselves or others for not having enough faith or not praying correctly or blame God as uncaring if they don't happen the way we wish? No. But we should be open when the Spirit prompts us to be part of the network of miracles God continues to work through the worldwide body of Christ!

PRAYER

Now for the great challenge of prayer (including prayer for healing and intercessory prayer). As I said in Chapter 1, my wrestling with questions about the character of God started with questions about prayer. If God already knows everything, why tell Him about our needs and situation? If God is perfectly good and wants the best for us, why try to persuade Him to do something? Do we try to get others to pray with us so that more prayers ascend to God? Will an increase in the number of prayers make Him be more willing to act? How does intercessory prayer work? Does my prayer for someone's salvation allow God to be more aggressive with that person? Do prayers get God to do more than He is already doing for someone? If so, is that fair to those who don't have anyone praying for them? Wouldn't it skew salvation in favor of some people?

As usual, we have to review our *nonnegotiable* anchor points: God is good. God wants the best. Our prayers will never talk God into becoming better than He already is. God is a constant; His love and forgiveness and grace are constants. God knows everything that can be known; His omniscience has no gaps. God always honors free choice; He'll never coerce anyone into faith, no matter how many people pray. Our prayers won't create heaven on earth.

What follows are some suggestions for a practical theology of prayer that preserves these nonnegotiable anchor points, deals honestly with the evidence about prayer that we observe in the real world, and avoids making prayer a mere self-help, psychological practice.

1. Prayer serves primarily to build our relationship with God. Prayer starts with "Our Father." To pray is to say "yes" to God's knocking on our door and to open the door to fellowship with Him (Revelation 3:20). It isn't asking the heavenly "genie" to do magic for us; it is basking and reveling in fellowship with the God of the universe, who said the night before He died, "I have called you friends" (John 15:15). So, prayer is primarily praise, worship, communication, listening, and just plain "being" with God.

2. God is a constant. He is already perfectly good, knows the good, and wants the good for us every moment. Within the limits of the great controversy, He is already working as hard as divinely possible for the salvation, growth, and quality of life of everyone. There is no "higher gear" for Him to shift into, no reserves to call into action, no software upgrade to install. So, why pray?

3. Prayer serves to change us, not God! This idea fits one of this book's themes: God is the constant, and we are the variable. Prayer can't make God more willing, better, or more active. Yet we are told to pray. So prayer must make *us* more willing, better, and more active! Ellen G. White wrote these famous lines:

> Prayer is not to work any change in God; it is to bring us into harmony with God.[1]
> Not that it is necessary in order to make known to God what we are, but in order to enable us to receive Him. Prayer does not bring God down to us, but brings us up to Him.[2]

Just as suggesting that the Cross was primarily meant to change God risks making certain negative implications about His character that none of us want to believe, so suggesting that prayer serves primarily to change God also involves certain negative implications about God with which few of us are comfortable. This idea would mean that God waits until someone prays before He'll "go into His highest gear." It would mean that He works harder for some than for others, which would be arbitrary and elitist. It would mean that if I can persuade Him of some good that He should accomplish, then I must have a better idea of the "good" than He does. If I must review for Him the "merits of the case," mustering various arguments to persuade Him, then He is forgetful or unaware. None of these ideas honors God.

4. Prayer dials us in to God's wisdom and power. God's grace, love, and wisdom are constants, like the sun and rain (Matthew 5:43-48). However, in the same way that people can choose to stay in the shade or to step into the sunlight, so they can choose whether or not to expose themselves to God's gifts. Prayer is that choice, exposing ourselves to God, "dialing in" to His gifts. We access all His gifts—grace and love and wisdom and power—through prayer. Radio and TV and other signals are flooding through every room, every car we're in, but we have to turn the dial to tune in the signal without static. In the same way, prayer is the process by which we tune in to God.

It's because of this matter of human choice, human will, that we earlier made the point that God's blessings are *indiscriminate externally* but *discriminate internally*. For God to skew His blessings in favor of Christians externally—to heal only Christians, to protect only tithe payers, to help only Christians survive wildfires, to bless Christians' stocks so that they soar far above all others, and to enable Christians to win all sporting events—would overwhelmingly weight the unbeliever's choice toward faith. Therefore, God has to send the sun and rain on both the just and the unjust. But prayer gives Him permission to pour His grace into our lives internally and spiritually. Prayer is like a faucet; it doesn't create the water or water pressure, but it controls the amount of flow. God's wisdom and counsel and grace are constants; prayer is the variable that determines how much of God's grace and love flow into our lives.

5. We can never use prayer to redefine the great controversy. God has drawn a line between good and evil (Revelation 7:1-4). He knows that if He crosses that line in using His power, He will overwhelm faith, or create "rice Christians,"* or risk coercing faith. Because He drew that

---

*If God gave every Christian a brand-new, blood-red Ferrari, my church would fill quickly—but for the wrong reason!

line with perfect wisdom and righteousness, we have to be very careful about asking Him to redraw that line to answer our particular prayers. In the cosmic great controversy between the forces of good and evil, He drew that line in that particular place for a reason, and I'm not sure I want to be the one to tell Him that He should have drawn it in another place! Leaving that line alone can be painful, because we want Him to make an exception in our particular case (for instance, heal my father in the ICU, or keep that truck from hitting him, or have him take his walk half an hour earlier). That's why we must pray the same prayer Christ prayed in the Garden, when He so desperately wanted to be free from the shadow of the Cross: " 'May this cup be taken from me. Yet not as I will, but as you will' " (see Matthew 26:37-43).

6. Prayer is more than merely psychological self-help or autosuggestion. Prayer is tremendously powerful! Think for a moment about the implications of the Lord's Prayer: We have a heavenly Father; He has a "will" for us and the world; He has the power to give us our daily bread; He can forgive. Faith believes that God hears and responds (Exodus 3:7-10).

However, we have also seen that God works mostly through people. He does His miracles primarily through the corporate body of Christ. So, the vast majority of the time He accomplishes His will by empowering people to be channels of His grace and power. Prayer opens our minds and souls, allowing God to pour grace and blessings on others through us.

God wants to hear our prayers. He loves to hear our hearts. Our prayers build a relationship, and that relationship certainly changes reality!

7. Prayer draws our will into agreement with God's will. If God's will is perfect but ours are still being sanctified, then God must be the constant and we must be the variables. Therefore, prayer is how we learn His will and learn to submit to it. Once we are living consciously, unconsciously, and instinctively in the center of His will, then we can do whatever we want because our will has become His will.[3] "Delight thyself also in the LORD; and he shall give thee the desires of thine heart" (Psalm 37:4, KJV).

In other words, the best way to get everything we ask for in our prayers is to pray for what God wants to give us! Buddhism suggests that people get rid of the pain of frustrated desires by getting rid of all sense of being a "self." Christianity agrees that disappointed desires contribute to suffering, but it suggests that the solution is not that we lose all sense of self, but rather that we align ourselves with God's will for our life. Then God is free to pour His will into us, and we can experience complete peace, satisfaction, and fulfillment.

8. God works through people to answer intercessory prayers. This may be the most challenging aspect of a theology of prayer; it nearly always stirs the most debate. Let's make a pledge of mutual respect as we wrestle to find a theology that is true to Scripture, that fits what most of us have experienced, that says nothing negative about God's character, and that preserves a powerful role for intercessory prayer!

Here's the challenge: If we assume that intercessory prayer persuades God to do something He wasn't willing to do before, that says negative things about God's goodness. The assumption that intercessory prayer gives God more leeway to convert people or to change the minds of authorities runs counter to our nonnegotiable anchor point that God never coerces, that God always respects free choice. The very popular traditional suggestion that intercessory prayer gives God "legal" permission in the great controversy with Satan to be more aggressive in saving people implies that God is somehow limited by Satan's authority in some areas or is bound by legal obstacles beyond His control. I don't think most of us want to suggest that. So, if we are correct in our nonnegotiable anchor points about God's character—that God is perfectly good, that He'll always respect free choice, that He isn't bound by any being or judicial constraints outside Himself, and that prayer primarily changes us rather than God—then we have to search for the reasons why God calls for us to pray intercessorily for others (Ephesians 6:18-20; 1 Thessalonians 1:2, 3).

As soon as we suggest that prayer primarily allows God to change us, to make us channels through which His life and grace can flow to others, people immediately get upset and imply we are suggesting that prayer is ineffective; that there is no reason to pray. *That's not the case at all!* Prayer is hugely powerful. Prayer makes a huge difference in the world. In the great controversy between good and evil, between Christ and Satan, God has chosen a line where the angels are holding back the winds of strife. God and all the beings in His divine army are arrayed against evil, against Satan and the demons (see Revelation 19:11ff; Ephesians 6:10ff).

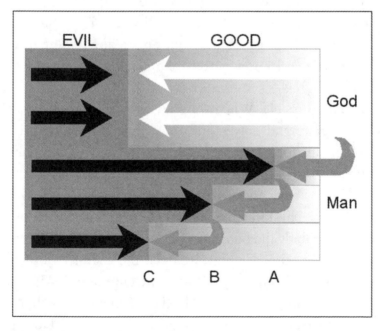

God's use of His power and of heavenly resources against evil is a constant. The prayers of believers, which free God to manifest His power through them as well (A, B, C), are the variable.

When we choose to step over the line and sign up as part of God's "army," we become partners with God in the battle against evil. Much of the time, God has chosen to exercise His power in the world through the collective body of Christ. He heals through the body, He distributes food and money through the body, and He makes His love and care real through the body. It should be obvious, then, that He also fights evil through the body. He "casts out demons" through the body of Christ. It is part of the mission of the church as the body of Christ to oppose evil everywhere it meets it, at every level, in every form.

Consequently, when we pray, we're not persuading God to move the line that He has drawn. God is a constant. Within the limits of the great controversy, He uses all His forces at full throttle all the time. He never sleeps. He never rests. He mobilizes the Holy Spirit and all the divine angels into the fray for each person at peak power, optimum efficiency, all the time! That line has been drawn in His infinite wisdom, and I don't want to be the one to suggest that I know better than He where that line should be drawn.

We are the variable! When we pray, we open ourselves as channels for His grace and power, and more power is released into the battle and Satan's forces are pushed back. The more Christians who open themselves to God's power and the more fully they open their talents and gifts and every pore of their being to be used by God, the further Satan and his kingdom are forced to retreat! We are opening our hearts and minds and bodies for God to use in His cosmic struggle against evil. Every time we pray, we open the channel a little more. And when a small group prays or an entire church prays or when all Christians pray, God has an incredibly larger arena in which to work. Evil is pushed back. Territory is retaken from Satan. Does prayer work? You bet! As Jack Provonsha says, "Prayer changes people, and people change things!"

What About Miracles and Prayer?

And, as we'll see in the closing chapter, even one individual can have an incredible amount of power and influence. But when that one individual is combined with the exponential scale of the entire body of Christ, huge advances can be made against evil.

As we noted earlier, Jesus said that His followers would do even greater things than He accomplished during His ministry here. It is prayer that unleashes this power. Our prayers do move God—not by changing His heart or character, but by giving Him room to work, to inspire, to empower, to mobilize, and to network resources in the great controversy against evil.

When someone drops a stone into a smooth pond, the ripples move out in concentric circles from "ground zero." The closer the ripples are to ground zero, the higher and more powerful they are. Though they decrease in size as they move away, they continue until they hit the shore. Tsunamis have pushed walls of water hundreds of feet high across thousands of miles of ocean!

When we pray, God changes us. Because I am in "solidarity" with many people, when I change, they cannot help but be affected to some degree. My changing affects my wife and my sons. It may also affect my pastoral staff, my congregation, and those who hear me on the radio. For instance, when we raise money for missions, we help missions and baptize people all around the world.

In the same way that the ripples are most powerful next to ground zero and least powerful at shore, so intercessory prayer has the most impact on ground zero. My prayers have the most effect on me and those closest to me. God pours life and wisdom and ideas and suggestions into my life that inspire me to do things I would not have done otherwise. But when my prayers are for needs distant from me, they have less impact. That seems clear when we look at the evidence. The vast majority of answered prayers are close by and immediate. Our prayers for the president may make a bit of an impact, but the evidence seems pretty clear that our prayers do not always result in the president making the kinds of choices that honor God! Our prayers have more impact locally than in China or India. We still pray for those places, and often God will lead us to start something that can make a difference even over there. But our prayers will not have as much immediate success in creating major changes in China or South Africa or elsewhere as they will in our immediate sphere of influence.

Doug Coe teaches people to persist in prayer.[4] He met a man named Bob who was thirty years old, a brand-new Christian. Bob wanted to learn more about prayer, so Doug told him, "Pick just one thing to pray about every day for six months. If God doesn't do something remarkable, I'll pay you $500. Thirty seconds or thirty minutes, I don't care. Just talk to God about this thing every day for six months."

Bob decided that he wanted to pray for a country; Kenya popped into his mind. He put a little post-it note by his bed and prayed for Kenya for five months. Nothing.

Then one night he was having dinner at some friends' house. Another guest asked him what he did. He said that he sold insurance and then asked, "What do you do?" She said she ran an orphanage—in Kenya.

Bob knew immediately that he was going to lose the $500! He spent the next hour asking this woman about Kenya. He could hardly breathe, knowing that God was at work. She finally said, "Bob, nobody ever, *ever* reacts like this. Do you want to fly over and see this orphanage?"

Bob did. And he became involved. He contacted pharmaceutical and medical supply companies about donating supplies for the orphanage. He met the president of Kenya, and led members of parliament to Christ. That's the power of prayer!

Intercessory prayer is also like the World Wide Web. The Web is made up of "nodes"—computer servers in universities or other centers that can handle a huge volume of messages. When we log on to the Internet to do a search, that search goes through the Web, sending messages, searching for information. Obviously, if one server goes down, then the Web is compromised a little bit. The more servers there are in the Web, the more impact it can make around the world.

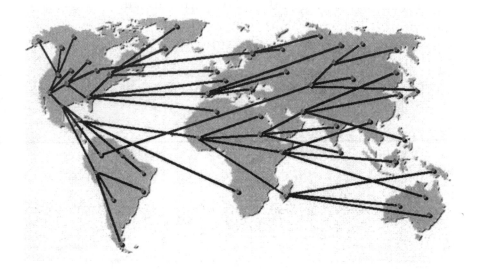

Intercessory prayer works the same way. The more Christians there are, the more "nodes" God has at His disposal to fight evil and to provide answers to prayer. God hears the prayers of millions of individuals, and each person praying is someone God can use to answer someone else's prayer. The resources of the Christian community fit the needs of the world. If we could just get everyone to pray and to be open to the Spirit, we could satisfy the needs of billions of people. The problem comes when people who have the resources to answer a particular need are not praying or listening, thus limiting the "miracles" God can do to answer the prayers of the needy.

Tony Campolo tells a story about a time when he went to speak at a Pentecostal college. In the back room, before he went on the platform, eight young future pastors knelt around him and laid their hands on him to pray for him. After a while Campolo began to get tired of them leaning on him and was hoping they'd finish soon. But one guy began to pray—not for Campolo, but for his neighbor: "God, you know my neighbor, Charlie Stolsis. He lives in that silver trailer a mile down the road, on the right. He left his wife and three kids this morning. God, do something. Lord, step in." Eventually the student finished praying, and Campolo gave his talk.

On his way home, Campolo picked up a hitchhiker. "What's your name?" he asked.

"Charlie Stolsis."

Campolo immediately drove off on an exit.

"Where are you going?" Charlie asked.

"I'm taking you home."

"Why are you doing that?"

"Because you just left your wife and your three kids—isn't that right?"

Charlie's eyes got big. "How did you know that?"

"God told me!"

Campolo drove right to the trailer. (A silver trailer, a mile down the road, on the right!)

"How did you know I live here?"

"God told me."

They walked in the front door, and Charlie's wife said, "You're back! You're back!" Charlie whispered to her, and her eyes got big! Then Campolo said, "You two sit down. I'm going to talk to you, and you're going to listen." He led them to Christ, and now Charlie's a pastor in California!

That's how prayer can work. God did a miracle! He put a burden on that young man next to Tony Campolo.

Yes, prayer works!

9. Prayers for healing **will** *be answered.* Scripture tells us to pray for healing (James 5:13-18), so we do. We anoint. And we celebrate all recoveries, all relief from pain. But a great deal of evidence points to the reality that prayers for healing are not guarantees.

We pray with the assumption that God is good, that He desires our good health and freedom from pain, and that He knows everything about the entire situation. He welcomes our prayers, but they don't add to His knowledge. However, these prayers, the mutual sharing of the pain of the situation, deepen the relationship.

We *don't* pray with the goal of persuading God to change His mind. We *don't* pray with the goal of trying to show Him that changing His "vote" in this case would be better than what He had planned. We *don't* have to present the merits of the case to God: "This is too much pain," "this person is too young," "they have so much more to do," and so on. God loves all equally! We *don't* pray in an attempt to avoid all the consequences of living in a world with random evil. We accept the fact that this world is submerged in a great controversy and that God has to allow evil in order to convince the universe of certain truths.

We *do* pray to tap into heavenly wisdom regarding how to handle the situation. We *do* pray for wisdom to select from various health professionals, institutions, and care plans or protocols. We *do* pray for growth in our understanding of the laws of health and for the grace and power to live by them! We *do* pray for the patience to endure the process of treatment.

We pray for spiritual life. We pray for grace, for forgiveness for ourselves and for others (James 5:13-17). Studies show a clear relationship between guilt, stress, and sickness. They also show the therapeutic value of a healthy spirituality, a purpose in living, peace, and rest.

We pray that the channel between us and God might be open. We pray that God will remove all obstacles in our soul or lifestyle that might be obstructing the free flow of grace into every part of our lives. We pray for a sense of joy and even for a sense of humor: "A merry heart doeth good like a medicine" (Proverbs 17:22, KJV).

When praying for others, we pray for God to use "community" for healing. Touch, love, acceptance, and empathy can be powerful channels for God's grace. If prayer changes us, then when we open ourselves to God in prayer for the healing of others, we give God more channels through which to express Himself. People experience God's touch and love through our touch and care.

We are willing to try every reasonable, reputable treatment plan. I have pastored individuals who refused scientific measures that doctors were clearly recommending. Some of these individuals said they did so because they wanted God to get all the credit. There may be good reasons to ask many questions, but to refuse widely accepted courses of treatment while asking God to do a miracle apart from all science is to attempt to force God to work out in the open when He is most comfortable working in the shadows.

C. S. Lewis tells a brief story. He got up one morning intending to get his hair cut in preparation for a visit to London. Then he received a letter that made it clear he didn't need to go to London, so he didn't need the haircut. But a nagging voice impressed him to get the haircut anyway, and when he walked in the door of the barbershop, the barber said, "I was praying you might come today." Lewis wrote, "Those who best know God will best know whether He sent me to the barber's shop because the barber prayed." God hides in the shadows to allow skeptics to doubt and people of faith to believe. He preserves free choice.[5]

God won't overwhelm faith or give people the wrong reasons to follow Him. When we're willing to undergo all reputable treatment options, when we live by the very best health principles and use effective natural remedies *along with prayer,* we allow God to work in the ways He wants to. If there is a miracle, it allows the person of faith to give credit and thanks to God while leaving the unbeliever free to disbelieve and credit science. This preserves free choice for all.

How then should we understand the very clear statement in James: "The prayer offered in faith will make the sick person well" (James 5:15)? The answer that I think best fits the evidence is that this promise assumes that the prayer is one of faith and is offered by a believer and that the other conditions in the passage and elsewhere in Scripture have been met. We can pray in absolute confidence that God will raise the sick person up. The *time factor* we leave to God. The sick person may be healed immediately (though that is obviously rare). He or she may begin to get better and, with appropriate medical treatment and care, recover in a few days or weeks or months. Or this person may not be healed until the resurrection morning, when God makes all things new. But the believing sick person *will* get well!

We are blessed every time someone gets well. We are blessed every time God steps into our world to intervene. We are blessed by the miracles that occur every day as the body of Christ networks to make a difference in the world. We are blessed by the "natural" miracles of love and babies and second chances in life and the promptings by the Spirit to write a note or send some money or help someone the very day that help is needed. But we wait for the complete fulfillment of the promise, "Whatever you ask in My name, that I will do" (John 14:13, NKJV). We wait for the day when we walk through the heavenly gates. May it be soon!

---

1. White, *Christ's Object Lessons*, 143.

2. White, *Steps to Christ*, 93.

3. White, *Desire of Ages*, 668.

4. John Ortberg, *If You Want to Walk on Water, You've Got to Get Out of the Boat* (Grand Rapids, Mich.: Zondervan, 2001), 91-93.

5. C. S. Lewis, *The World's Last Night and Other Essays by C. S. Lewis* (New York: Harcourt Brace Jovanovich, 1960), 3, 8.

CHAPTER ELEVEN

How Will the Wicked Die the Second Death?

A note from the author: In this chapter I've attempted to wrestle honestly with one of the most challenging questions about the character of God. I offer the thoughts that follow as a tentative solution that stands open to refinement, revision, and correction by those much more knowledgeable than I am. I welcome dialogue that's offered in a spirit of grace and love in a shared search for both unity and an understanding of divine truth.

How will the wicked die at the end of the world? How can a gracious, forgiving God destroy people with fire? But if God doesn't kill them, how will they die?

In the rest of this book, we will deal with some of the difficult questions about the character of God that have to do with "eschatology," or last-day events. One of the most difficult is, How can God destroy people at the end? No decent parents anywhere would be willing to destroy their own children, no matter how evil they are. They would all beg for a life sentence, for healing, for counseling, for another chance, or for banishment, but not for death and never death at their own hand. So, how can we believe that God, the Father of all fathers, the Parent of all parents, would do so?

The traditional view has been that God is a holy, sin-hating God. His holiness, His honor, and His justice demand that sin, being so incredibly offensive to His purity, must have the maximum penalty, eternal death. But God's justice is matched by an even greater love, so He sent His only Son to die that death in our place. All who accept that death in their place will escape the second death; the death angel will "pass over" them. But all those who refuse to paint the blood of Christ over the door of their hearts will experience the second death at the hand of God Himself in His final "strange act."

While people have promoted a great variety of views on the sequence of events leading up to the Second Coming, the millennium, the nature of hell, and how long the fire will burn, most have pictured God, in the end, destroying those who reject His grace. But if the alternative model we've looked at is true—that God is *not* one who can destroy forever His own children; that He is, once and forever, the gentle, gracious God of Christmas and the Cross; a Person no one need ever fear—then how will God ever rid the universe of evil?

In chapter three of this book I suggested that we find the major theological fork in the road, the continental divide, at the Tree in the Garden. Our view of what happened at the Tree has powerful implications for what we are likely to believe about the Cross and what we believe will happen to the wicked at the end of the world. For those who believe that at the Tree, God threatened divine punishment for sin, it is logical that at the Cross, God the Father was killing Christ in our place, and it logically follows then that if the wicked reject that substitutionary death, God will destroy them at the end of the world.

If, on the other hand, we believe that at the Tree God was giving a loving warning about the natural consequences of sin (separation from God), it seems logical to see the Cross as God the Father and Christ together experiencing in our place the natural consequences of sin (wrenching separation from each other). That would also imply that the wicked will die at the end of the world, *not* by the hand of God, but rather as the natural consequence of choosing to live apart from the Father, the only Source of life in the universe. With a breaking heart, God, who highly values and always honors free choice, no longer "forces" His life, love, and grace on them; He "gives them up" (Romans 1:24).

The challenge is that, on the surface, inspired statements seem to support each of the options. That's why we spent an entire chapter on hermeneutics and the hard questions of the Old Testament. Somehow, we have to find a model or a theology that (1) is true to Inspiration; (2) is true to the nonnegotiable anchor points about God's character that are crystal clear in Scripture; and (3) offers credible interpretations of the statements that at first glance seem to support the other view.

Every single doctrine about God has to be true to His essential core character. There can be no rogue doctrines! All that we say about God has to be good news and give life more abundantly. Jesus Christ is the same yesterday, today, and forever (Hebrews 13:8). He is love forever. He is faithful—*chesed*—forever. He wants no relationship or worship motivated by fear, ever. He spreads His sunshine of grace, love, and forgiveness on all, everywhere, all the time. Can we find some answers about the last days that are consistent with those nonnegotiable anchor points?

IMPLICATIONS OF THE CROSS

If Jesus is always the last word on the truth about God and if His death on the Cross is the supreme revelation of His testimony about God and if He died the second death on the Cross in our place—the eternal death of the wicked who reject Jesus—then we can and *must* look to the Cross to determine our theology of last-day events.

How did Jesus die? Did God kill Him? Jesus made it very clear, twice, that it was not the Father who killed Him. He said, " 'I lay down my life. . . . No one takes it from Me' " (see John 10:17, 18). And on the Cross He cried out, " 'My God, my God, why have you forsaken me?' " (Matthew 27:46). Jesus made it clear that, after eons of being absolutely together as One, He was experiencing the torture of having His relationship with the Father ripped apart. But the Father was not killing Him. He begged His Father to forgive. He released His Spirit to His Father. God was not killing Christ. That should give us reason to question the assumption that God will destroy the wicked at the end.

If it is true that on the Cross Jesus endured the wrath of the Father, then we have to ask what the Bible means by that wrath. Romans 1 seems to clearly say that when God "exercises" His wrath, He gives the wicked over to the natural consequences of their own choices. God respects their free choice enough to let them go. That fits what we see at the Tree in the Garden, in the story of the prodigal son, and at the Cross. God said to Israel, " 'How can I give you up, Ephraim? How can I hand you over, Israel?' " (Hosea 11:8). Paul said that at the Cross, Jesus "was delivered over to death for our sins" (Romans 4:25).

Jürgen Moltmann said that Jesus experienced being "abandoned" by God.[1] In Gethsemane and on the Cross, He could no longer experience, at any level of His being, the presence of the Father. Nor could the Father experience the Son. Together they went through what Abraham and Isaac went through on Mount Moriah. And they went through what the wicked and God will experience at the end: wrenching separation, caused by the natural consequences of sin.

One of the initial triggers to my study of this doctrine was a set of quotations that someone shared with me. The quotations, from the books *Desire of Ages* and *The Great Controversy,* seemed to view the end of the wicked as a natural consequence rather than a direct divine punishment. Here they are:

> God does not stand toward the sinner as an executioner of the sentence against transgression; but He leaves the rejecters of His mercy to themselves, to reap that which they have sown. Every ray of light rejected, every warning despised or unheeded, every passion indulged, every transgression of the law of God, is a seed sown which yields its unfailing har-

vest. The Spirit of God, persistently resisted, is at last withdrawn from the sinner, and then there is left no power to
control the evil passions of the soul, and no protection from
the malice and enmity of Satan. The destruction of Jerusalem
is a fearful and solemn warning to all who are trifling with
the offers of divine grace and resisting the pleadings of divine
mercy. Never was there given a more decisive testimony to
God's hatred of sin and to the certain punishment that will
fall upon the guilty.[2]

When He [Christ] leaves the sanctuary, darkness covers
the inhabitants of the earth. In that fearful time the righteous
must live in the sight of a holy God without an intercessor.
The restraint which has been upon the wicked is removed,
and Satan has entire control of the finally impenitent. God's
long-suffering has ended. The world has rejected His mercy,
despised His love, and trampled upon His law. The wicked
have passed the boundary of their probation; the Spirit of
God, persistently resisted, has been at last withdrawn.
Unsheltered by divine grace, they have no protection from
the wicked one. Satan will then plunge the inhabitants of the
earth into one great, final trouble. As the angels of God cease
to hold in check the fierce winds of human passion, all the
elements of strife will be let loose. The whole world will be
involved in ruin more terrible than that which came upon
Jerusalem of old.

A single angel destroyed all the first-born of the Egyptians and filled the land with mourning. . . . The same destructive power exercised by holy angels when God commands,
will be exercised by evil angels when He permits. There are
forces now ready, and only waiting the divine permission, to
spread desolation everywhere.[3]

How Will the Wicked Die the Second Death?

This is not an act of arbitrary power on the part of God. The rejecters of His mercy reap that which they have sown. God is the fountain of life; and when one chooses the service of sin, he separates from God, and thus cuts himself off from life. He is "alienated from the life of God." Christ says, "All they that hate Me love death." Eph. 4:18; Prov. 8:36. God gives them existence for a time that they may develop their character and reveal their principles. This accomplished, they receive the results of their own choice.[4]

The context of these quotations reveals that while all three refer to events at the end of the world, the first two are premillennial, picturing the time before the Second Coming when God withdraws His restraining power and the forces of evil destroy each other. It seems that all would agree that this destruction is the result of God's "giving them up" to natural consequences.

The third quotation clearly refers to the postmillennial destruction of the wicked. It seems to imply that that destruction also does not result from God's direct use of "arbitrary power," but rather is the natural consequence of the choice of the wicked. I will have to leave to each reader to decide whether these quotations comprise a pattern indicating that Ellen White believed that we should not view God as the initiator of the destruction in either judgment.

VIEWS ON THE DEATH OF THE WICKED

When I first came across these quotes, I was shocked! And, logically, I had to ask the question, If God doesn't destroy the wicked in the second death, then how will they die? Surely they don't commit collective voluntary suicide! To answer that question, let me put it in context of some of the traditional views on hell and the end of the wicked:

Eternal hellfire: The Roman Catholic tradition has pictured a literal, eternally burning hellfire, where the wicked are sent and are kept alive to experience the torture as punishment for daring to oppose and disobey God. It also pictures a purgatory where people can have their sins purged so they can eventually go to heaven.

The mainstream Protestant tradition rejected purgatory but retained the idea of hellfire. It says that when lost people die, they go straight to hell and experience the torture of being burned continually, without relief, forever.

Annihilation of the wicked: The traditional Seventh-day Adventist position has been to reduce hell to a very brief period, perhaps even a moment. The fires are still a punishment from God, His "strange act," but they are mercifully brief; the wicked and Satan and all the demons are destroyed, never to live again. The fires of hell burn until all vestiges of sin are removed and the world is cleansed, ready for the creation of the new earth. This view is much more consistent with Scripture and with the picture of a gracious God. He's not the kind of God who would punish His "children" with the torture of fire forever for sinning just one solitary time—for coloring outside the lines a single time.

In his autobiography, Merv Griffin wrote that occasionally he would broadcast his variety TV show from Caesar's Palace in Las Vegas. One day he saw a booth where a quarter would buy a view of a chicken dancing. Merv thought that was pretty funny and asked the owner of the booth to bring his act to the variety show.

When the man showed up for the rehearsal, he asked an attendant if they had an electrical outlet on the set.

"Why do you need an outlet?"

"For my hot plate."

"Why do you need a hot plate?"

"What do you think makes the chicken dance?"

They turned the guy in to the Society for the Prevention of Cruelty to Animals.

How Will the Wicked Die the Second Death?

Here's the point: If even Las Vegas can figure out that no one should do that to *animals,* how can Christians believe that God tortures *people?* No, God isn't like that, and I'm proud to be part of a tradition that has stood tall for telling the truth about God. A number of key evangelical figures have moved in this direction over the past few years.[5] However, many of us have wondered if we might be able to increase even further our understanding of exactly how the wicked will die and how evil will be eradicated from the universe once and for all without compromising the biblical picture of God as a God of love.

Destroyed by God's glory: Another variation has been to focus on the idea suggested by 2 Thessalonians 2:8: "The Lord shall consume [the antichrist] with the spirit of his mouth, and shall destroy [him] with the brightness of his coming" (KJV). Ellen G. White uses the same concept in *Desire of Ages:* "By a life of rebellion, Satan and all who unite with him place themselves so out of harmony with God that His very presence is to them a consuming fire. The glory of Him who is love will destroy them."[6]

In this model, God is not seen as actually actively punishing the wicked. God simply comes in all His holy glory, and sin and evil cannot exist in the presence of the holy glory of God. He is not actively destroying, but simply being Himself, being "God," and the natural consequences occur.

Wicked are already dead before the Fire: A third variation suggests that when God sends the fires traditionally associated with hell and the lake of fire, the wicked have already died. Rather than punishing and torturing the wicked, the fire purifies the earth, erasing all the results of sin and preparing for the recreation of the new earth.

This model fits best with the idea that God was warning of natural consequences at the Tree and that He did not destroy His own Son on the Cross. At the Tree, at the Cross, and at the end of the world, the wicked experience the natural consequences of choosing to live apart from God. He is proven to be a God of love and grace who *never* treats sinners as Satan warned them He would, but *always* gives grace and healing.*

HOW THE WICKED DIE

So, to summarize—how will the wicked die?

1. *They die because they have voluntarily disconnected themselves from the Source of life.* As surely as pulling the plug makes the TV go black, so the lost will stop breathing when God honors their decision to disconnect from Him. God has spent thousands of years giving life to those whose choices still hung in the balance. Even when they may have indicated that they were diametrically opposed to God, He continued to give them life, pursuing them through the Holy Spirit, pouring out grace and love, drawing them to Himself. He worked day and night with all the resources of the universe.

However, when they have repeatedly made clear that they want nothing to do with God, He finally, with a breaking heart, removes His life-giving power. He stops pursuing. That is His "strange act," because it is completely foreign to His nature. As Jesus cried, "O Jerusalem, Jerusalem, thou that killest the prophets, and stonest them which are sent unto thee, how often would I have gathered thy children together, even as a hen gathereth her chickens under her wings, and ye would not!" (Matthew 23:37, KJV). Here we have pictured God's desire, His pursuing, and their rejection. God honors their final decision.

Some people ask, "What's the difference between God killing and God withdrawing? The result is the same: People still die."

Yes, God's withdrawal or "abandonment" is a volitional act. But surely letting people make their own choice is not morally equivalent

---

*While this model allows us to interpret the Tree, the Cross, and the Fire with consistency and while it preserves God as a God who never acts contrarily to His love and life-giving nature, it has certainly troubled a number of Christian scholars and laypersons alike because of the statements that seem to be in conflict. It certainly is a subject about which conscientious people can disagree. Hopefully, we can continue the dialogue with mutual love and respect!

to actively destroying them! It is an act of love, honoring free choice, which is radically different than destroying those who have rejected God's love. God still loves the lost. He still has eternally forgiven the lost. But He withdraws His life and presence, as He did in the Garden of Gethsemane and on the Cross.

2. They die to escape "torment." When Christ encountered the two demoniacs, the demons within them immediately cried out, " 'What do you want with us, Son of God? . . . Have you come here to torture us before the appointed time?' " (Matthew 8:29) The Greek word translated "torture" appears also in the third angel's message: "He, too, will drink of the wine of God's fury, which has been poured full strength into the cup of his wrath. He will be tormented with burning sulfur in the presence of the holy angels and of the Lamb. And the smoke of their torment rises for ever and ever. There is no rest day or night" (Revelation 14:9-11).

Evidently, the holiness and purity of Christ strikes hard-core, fully developed, demonized people like fiery torture. Matthew 8 mentions no fire, but to the demons, being in Christ's presence felt like fire. Think of the torment people experienced on the top floors of the World Trade Center on September 11; it was so terrible that they chose to jump rather than endure it! These demons felt that kind of torment in the presence of Christ. That is the natural consequence hardened sinners experience in the presence of the love and grace of Jesus Christ. Perhaps that is also something like the torment the wicked will feel in the presence of Christ when they see Him face to face at His second coming. It will hurt worse than fire.

The third angel's message says that the wicked know "no rest day or night." But Christ invites us all: "Come to me, . . . and I will give you rest" (Matthew 11:28). If we come to Christ, we will receive rest. If we reject Christ, we will have no rest.

This perspective explains Revelation 6:16, where the wicked are pictured as calling for the rocks and mountains to fall on them. When the lost are in the presence of Christ and they see incredible love and grace in His face, they will realize what they have eternally lost. In a horrible instant, they will realize what an incredibly terrible choice they have made. They will have lost Pascal's wager.* Either the emotional torment will crush their soul or they will call for the rocks and mountains to fall upon them to put them out of their agony.

This is how and why Christ died. He did not die because of the physical pain caused by the spear, the nails, the beating, and the thorns. "Christ felt the anguish which the sinner will feel. . . . The sense of sin . . . broke the heart of the Son of God."[7] "He bore the guilt of transgression, and the hiding of His Father's face, until His heart was broken and His life crushed out."[8]

3. Some of the wicked may destroy each other. It is in the very nature of evil to destroy. That's why God's angels must hold back the winds of strife (Revelation 7:1-3). It is why Paul said that nature is groaning under the bondage of sin (Romans 8). When God removes His restraining power, all nature goes berserk (Revelation 6:12-17)[9] and evil is free to do what it will. In the same way that in the famous parable the scorpion stings the frog that is carrying it across the river "because it is in my nature," so it is in demonic human nature to destroy. Ellen White wrote:

> I was shown that the judgments of God would not come directly out from the Lord upon them, but in this way: They place themselves beyond His protection. . . . If they choose their own way, then He does not commission His angels to prevent Satan's decided attacks upon them.[10]

---

*Pascal suggested that it seems only wise and prudent to "bet" on Christ rather than against Him. If we choose for Christ and then, when life ends, discover that eternal life doesn't exist, we wouldn't have lost much. Choosing Christ brings many practical benefits. But if we "bet" against Christ and at the end of life discover that was a mistake, we'd suffer a terrible loss. We'd miss out on heaven and God and fellowship and life and creativity and sensual experiences beyond imagining—forever! See Blaise Pascal, *Pensees* (New York: Penguin Books, 1966), 153.

How Will the Wicked Die the Second Death?

In Thailand, people raise fighting fish. They put two of them in the same tank, separated by a glass wall. The fish circle for days, eyeing each other. When all the bets are on the table, the bettors raise the restraining glass wall, and the fish fight to the death. Similarly, God is holding back evil today. In the last days, He'll withdraw His restraining power, and those who have chosen evil will destroy each other.

The Old Testament contains numerous examples of this. In the famous battle of Jehoshaphat, the army did not fight; instead they put the choir in the front and worshiped God! The next morning, all their enemies were dead; they had killed each other (see 2 Chronicles 20). When Gideon led Israel, God caused the Midianites to kill each other (Judges 7). Revelation 17 indicates that when the kings of the whole world realize that the prostitute/antichrist has duped them, they turn on her. Evil kills evil.* Millions will die in these brutal slaughters. The Fire will cleanse and wipe the slate clean.

GOD NEVER CHANGES

Another thread of support for the idea that God will not be the One to actively destroy the wicked at the second death comes from the evidence that God never changes from His core character. The destruction of the wicked is often referred to as God's "strange act" because if He were to destroy all who have rebelled against Him and rejected the grace flowing from the Cross of His own Son, that act would seem to contradict the rest of the record regarding God's character.

One afternoon when I was wrestling with the verse that speaks of the wicked being slain by the brightness of God's glory, I began to mull over exactly what His glory comprises. I had read C. S. Lewis' famous sermon "The Weight of Glory,"[11] in which he makes clear that God's glory is not yellow "luminosity." We have always understood that God's glory stands for His character. Lewis makes a great

---

*See also 1 Samuel 14:20; 2 Kings 3:23; Ezekiel 38:21; Haggai 2:22; Zechariah 14:13.

case for God's glory being His approval, His "Well done," His "Yes" spoken to each person who is saved.

Paul wrote that Satan has blinded the minds of men to "the light of the gospel of the glory of Christ, who is the image of God" (2 Corinthians 4:4). Then he went on: "God, who said, 'Let light shine out of darkness,' made his light shine in our hearts to give us the light of the knowledge of the glory of God in the face of Christ" (verse 6). So the glory of God is seen best in the face of Christ.

Christ said He was the light of the world (John 8:12). He said He came to reveal the Father. He said He had done what He had been sent to do, which was to bring glory to the Father (John 17:1-5). This glory, the glory of Christ, the glory of God, is the gospel, the good news. That should be a powerful clue to us as to what the wicked will see when they see the face of Christ at His return!

David repeatedly asked God to turn His face toward His people. He knew that this meant approval, love, and justice: God ruling in favor of His people. During the air raids of World War II, a little girl and her father were spending the night on cots in a subway tunnel. Unable to sleep, the girl asked her father, "Are you right there?" After repeated assurances that he was there and encouragements to go to sleep, she had to ask once more, "But, Daddy, is your face turned toward me?" God's face turned toward us stands for His approval, His care, His love.

Clearly, the "glory" of God is not some previously unknown harsh, vindictive side of Him. This glory that is seen in the face of Christ is a continuation of what God has always been and what Christ came to reveal: grace, love, forgiveness, and acceptance.

Martin Luther struggled because he believed the righteousness of God spoken of in Romans 1:17 was God's holy and punishing wrath against sin and sinners. Theologians say Luther's "tower experience" was the moment when he was converted from this view to viewing God's righteousness as the love and forgiveness He gives us apart from works. In the same way, our understanding of God's glory on the clouds has to be guided by these clear texts.

When the righteous and the wicked see the face of Christ (God) on the clouds at His second coming, what will they see? When He comes with His sickle in His hand to reap the harvest (Rev. 14:13ff), what will we see in His face? The glory of Christ. The character of God. It will be what it has always been—life-giving love and grace. He has not changed from the Christmas Christ or the Cross Christ. He is forever the same. "It will be seen that the glory shining in the face of Jesus is the glory of self-sacrificing love."[12]

As I continued to mull over what the wicked would see in the face of Christ, I thought of Peter. What did he see in Christ's face immediately after he denied Him three times?

> Peter's eyes were drawn to his Master. In that gentle countenance he read deep pity and sorrow, but there was *no anger there.*
>
> The sight of that pale, suffering face, those quivering lips, that *look of compassion and forgiveness, pierced his heart like an arrow.* . . . Once more he looked at his Master, and saw a sacrilegious hand raised to smite Him in the face. Unable longer to endure the scene, he rushed, *heartbroken,* from the hall. . . . It was torture to his bleeding heart to know that he had added the heaviest burden to the Saviour's humiliation and grief. On the very spot where Jesus had poured out His soul in agony to His Father, Peter fell upon his face, and *wished that he might die.*[13]

If anyone deserved "wrath" and anger, it was Peter. He had stoutly rebuked Jesus for suggesting that he could ever possibly deny Him. Then he had point-blank, that very night, denied Him. Yet Christ's face showed no anger, only compassion and forgiveness. That is all that the wicked will ever see in the face of Christ on the clouds. That is the glory the wicked will see. And it will cause them to be "heartbroken"; it will "pierce their heart like an arrow," and they will rush out, "wishing that they might die."

PRIMARY AND SECONDARY CAUSATION

One of the great challenges we face in studying this subject is the diversity of statements in Scripture and the writings of Ellen G. White (see Chapter 7, on the principles of interpretation). In the statements I've quoted above, it seems clear that Mrs. White took great care to defend God's character, to state that He does not execute the lost. Other statements, however, suggest that it is God Himself who rains fire down from heaven to punish the wicked.

One concept that might help release at least some of the tension between these sets of quotations is the differentiation between primary and secondary causation. Revelation 15 pictures the saints standing on the sea of glass, victorious over the beast and his image. It says, "They held harps given them by God and sang the song of Moses the servant of God and the song of the Lamb" (verses 2, 3). Obviously these songs are last-day songs, sung to honor the character of God (see verses 3, 4) and to celebrate the great victory He has achieved for them.

As I thought about this, it seemed logical to go back to Exodus 15 to consider the roots of the song of Moses. God had just delivered the children of Israel from the Egyptians at the Red Sea. The parallels are obvious: They'd been in captivity for a long time. Someone had come to deliver them. They were saved from death only by being under the blood of a lamb.

Now their survival seemed unlikely. With the Red Sea before them, mountains on each side, and the enemy behind them, they were trapped. But God worked a miracle—Moses "stretched out his hand," the waters piled up, and the people crossed over on dry land. When the Egyptians pursued them into this path through the Red Sea, Moses stretched out his hand again, the waters returned to their natural place, and the Egyptians died.

How Will the Wicked Die the Second Death?

And what did Moses, Miriam, and the others sing, as they picked up their tambourines to celebrate after the great victory? "I will sing to the LORD, for he is highly exalted. The horse and its rider he has hurled into the sea" (Exodus 15:1; see also verse 21). What about that word *hurled?* There's no *hurling* in the story!

God worked a miracle to give the Israelites "life." When they were safely on the other side, He "relaxed" the miracle, He "allowed" the waters to return, and the Egyptians were at the wrong place at the wrong time. But in the Israelites' mind and theology, God was sovereign over everything. They credited everything that happened to God.* And so in their poetry and exuberance, they said God "hurled" the Egyptians into the sea. In reality, He simply withdrew the miracle He had worked to give the Israelites life and safety, and He allowed the Egyptians to die as the natural consequence of being in the wrong place at the wrong time.

The church has long known that to preserve the integrity of God's character, we have to understand many of the active verbs in the Bible in a more passive sense: What the Bible says God "did" often means what God "allowed." God didn't send an evil spirit into Saul so that he'd hurl the javelin at David; God allowed it. God doesn't send a strong delusion so that the wicked will believe a lie (see 2 Thessalonians 2:10-12); He allows it.

In theology and philosophy, this distinction is known as the difference between *primary* and *secondary causation*. The term *primary causation* refers to someone's intentional act; it would apply if God were to actively destroy the wicked. The term *secondary causation* refers to an action that only indirectly produces a result; for instance, when God withdraws His power in respect of people's own voluntary, insistent choice, and they die. The result is the same, but the moral factor is decisively different. So we have to look at the context to try to understand in each case whether God is actively doing something or whether it is more passive: allowing or withdrawing.

---

*For further discussion of this point, see Thompson, *Inspiration,* 173ff.

The saints pictured in Revelation 15 are singing a magnificent tribute to the character of God. Their song says that He's been able to save His people, to bring them across the "Red Sea" over to the Promised Land on the other side, without having to compromise His essential character. He destroyed nobody in the Red Sea crossing, and He will destroy nobody in the eschatological crossing over to the ultimate Promised Land.

God will win the great controversy and cleanse the universe of evil using only those methods consistent with His character: goodness, love, and truth. He gives only life. He refuses to use His power to hurt or punish in any ultimate sense. He doesn't actively cause any to die the second, eternal death. Whether it's the Egyptians or the lost at the end of time, people die only when they force God, because of their choice, to withhold His life-giving power.

This model allows us to maintain God as a constant, always the same, always gracious, loving, and forgiving. He is safe forever. You can always afford to "draw near." Even on the day when the wicked die the second death, all those watching will see that God is still absolutely trustworthy. They can love, worship, and be comfortable with Him forever because they have seen His character. That's why the saints on the sea of glass sing the song of Moses and of the Lamb!

---

1. Jürgen Moltmann, *The Crucified God* (Minneapolis: Fortress, 1993), 205.

2. White, *Great Controversy*, 36.

3. Ibid., 614.

4. White, *Desire of Ages*, 764.

5. See, e.g., John Stott and David L. Edwards, *Evangelical Essentials* (Downers Grove, Ill.: InterVarsity Press, 1988), 312-319; and Robert Peterson, "Undying Work, Unquenchable Fire," *Christianity Today*, October 21, 2000, 30-37.

6. White, *Desire of Ages*, 764.

7. Ibid., 753.

8. White, *Great Controversy*, 540.

9. Ibid., 614.

10. White, *Manuscript Releases*, (Silver Spring, Md.: E. G. White Estate, 1993), 14:3.

11. C. S. Lewis, *The Weight of Glory and Other Addresses* (New York: Macmillan, 1980), 3-19.

12. White, *Desire of Ages*, 20.

13. Ibid., 712, 713 (emphasis added).

CHAPTER TWELVE

Last-Day Events and the Book of Revelation

Why has Jesus waited so long to come back? How can "soon" mean two thousand years? How can a God of love send the seals, trumpets, and plagues of Revelation? Do we have to go through a time without a mediator? Why does God have a millennium and then bring all the wicked back to life again?

Now that we've come nearly to the end of this book, maybe it's time to deal with the end of THE Book! We've wrestled with character-of-God questions at the Tree, the Cross, and the Fire. We've looked at the questions of evil and suffering. Now let's deal with the last days; let's get into the great and wonderful and mysterious book of Revelation.*

Every religion wrestles with questions about the future and life after death. Every religion wrestles with the issue of how to avoid going to hell. Christianity believes in a very real and tangible heaven and new earth rather than a nirvana or purely spirit world. We believe that we can settle our eternal destiny in one lifetime rather than to suffer through thousands or millions of reincarnations before improving our karma enough to achieve nirvana. We believe that heaven

---

*There are many books out there that deal exclusively with eschatology and last-day events. This one chapter cannot cover it all. Marvin Moore, Morris Venden, Dwight Nelson, Jon Paulien, and Steve Wohlberg have all provided excellent resources within the recent Adventist tradition.

means living forever face to face with God, as close as if we were the only ones present. We believe that a place beyond imagination has been prepared for us. We know that heaven will be the party to end all parties, the vacation to end all vacations.

Ultimately, however, we want to be in heaven because of what we believe God is really like—that He is not like what His enemies have pictured Him to be. We've weighed the evidence and decided that He is the kind of God with whom we could spend forever. He is the lover in the Song of Solomon. It will be a delight forever to be in His presence. C. S. Lewis says that we will recognize all of our beloveds in the Beloved.[1] Every spoon of Coldstone ice cream, every minute on the beaches of Hawaii, every experience of intimate love—these all have been only a dim taste of the joy of living with God forever.

But if God is a lover who longs to be with His bride, why has He left her waiting for two thousand years?

THE DELAY

The first question we have to ask is, Has God set a date arbitrarily? Are we simply waiting for the clock of the universe to strike midnight? Or is the date "contingent"?

A while ago, a delegation came see me. These people had calculated that Christ would come at some point between the new millennium and 2003. They had based their calculations on the seventy Jubilee cycles and the six days of Creation. They reasoned that since Scripture says that in God's eyes a day is like a thousand years, the six days of Creation represent the six thousand years of this world's existence. Therefore we were about to enter the seventh thousand-year period— God's Sabbath rest! They believed that God was going to reach a point where He simply wouldn't put up with the delay any longer and would arbitrarily initiate the final events leading up to the Second Coming.

I tried to challenge them gently by suggesting that if God could choose the date arbitrarily, regardless of events or conditions on this earth (contingency), that He is at least partly responsible for the terrible suffering that's happened during the delay—between the time Jesus *could* have come and the time He actually *did* come. If He could have come in the first century and chose arbitrarily to come in the twenty-first century, wouldn't that make Him partly responsible for all the massacres, for the black plague, the Inquisition, the Crusades, the twenty million killed under Stalin, and the six million under Hitler? I shared my belief that God is never arbitrary and that if He were simply going to choose a time, Jesus would almost certainly have returned immediately after His ascension. He is a lover, not willing be to be separated from His beloved five minutes more than absolutely necessary.

In understanding the delay, then, we have to find a careful balance between God's sovereignty, that He is ultimately in control of everything in the universe, and His absolute commitment to free choice. God has chosen to share power in the universe, and therefore there is contingency and surprise and uncertainty. Yes, God is working in our world to bring events to closure and the outcome is absolutely certain. But He has chosen to do so in partnership with the church, the Body of Christ, and He is constantly opposed by incredibly powerful and intelligent demonic powers who work day and night to frustrate His will.

So, if God hasn't arbitrarily chosen a date for Jesus' return, what is He waiting for? The traditional answers are (1) for the gospel of the kingdom to be preached in all the world (Matthew 24:14); (2) for "the character of Christ [to] be perfectly reproduced in His people"[2]; or (3) for the "cup of iniquity" to become full.[3]

1. Gospel commission: Certainly the most traditional answer has been that God is waiting for the gospel to be preached to all the world. That belief has motivated thousands of missionaries to leave home and pour out their lives in sharing the gospel. At a General Conference session in San Francisco when I was a toddler learning to walk, my parents responded to an appeal to go to the mission field. They spent fifteen incredible years in Thailand.

But this answer raises some legitimate questions: Does it make Christ's coming dependent on the church? Will the gospel ever be preached to every human being on earth since more people are being born all the time? Which gospel has to be preached? Is each denomination a legitimate witness, or must a particular (Adventist) form of the gospel be preached to the whole world? Do people have to hear it directly from a person or does radio count? The Internet? Books? A handbill in the mail? A notice in the newspaper? And how much do people have to hear—all the doctrines of our church? All good questions.

2. Harvest principle: The idea that God is waiting for a critical mass of followers of Christ to reproduce the character of Christ perfectly has been called the "harvest principle." Those who hold this idea claim that God is waiting for a group of people to "ripen" spiritually so that they model to the universe what people totally committed to God look like. They show that people *can* live holy, godly lives in a pagan world and prove that God was telling the truth when He said that they can.

Yes, God has chosen to put His reputation on the line through the church, and He does call the church to reflect His character to the world. Those who disagree with this model, though, fear that it leads to perfectionism, pressure, guilt, and a very human-centered focus on what *we* have to do to speed up Christ's return.

3. Cup of iniquity: The third common option is that God is waiting for the "cup of iniquity" to be filled. He is waiting for Satan to demonstrate fully the disastrous consequences of living apart from God and sinning. Iniquity will finally "redline"; it will reach the limit God has set, and then He'll step in to keep evil from totally destroying the world.

The question is, Hasn't there already been enough evil in the world? Weren't World War II and Hitler enough? What does God have to see before His tolerance for evil reaches its limit? If taken to an extreme, this model can make it appear that God is partly responsible for allowing ongoing evil because His limit (inconceivably) has not been met.

Which option is the real reason for the delay? Many would say that there is truth in all three. The great controversy model ties all three together.

THE GREAT-CONTROVERSY/CHARACTER-OF-GOD MODEL

The gospel that must go to the whole world is the good news about what God is truly like, that He's a God of grace and love. The great controversy can't be brought to closure until that message has gone to every living human being. God couldn't bear to bring down the final curtain until every person has had an adequate opportunity to know the truth about Him. To have people reject Him based on a distorted view of His character would be hugely unfair. And so, yes, the gospel needs to go to the whole world.

It is the darkness of misapprehension of God that is enshrouding the world. Men are losing their knowledge of His character. It has been misunderstood and misinterpreted. At this time a message from God is to be proclaimed, a message illuminating in its influence and saving in its power. His character is to be made known. Into the darkness of the world is to be shed the light of His glory, the light of His goodness, mercy, and truth. . . . The last rays of merciful light, the last message of mercy to be given to the world, is a revelation of His character of love. The children of God are to manifest His glory. In their own life and character they are to reveal what the grace of God has done for them.[4]

The final message that will go around the world (Revelation 18:1-4) is the truth about God. The final showdown will be about God, about who is telling the truth. The date that God sets is based on the moment when every being in the universe has had a quality opportunity to know the truth about God and has made a voluntary, informed, settled choice for or against Him.

This theme ties the other three together. The gospel that is to be preached in all the world is the good news about God, that He is constantly and forever kind, gracious, loving, forgiving, and merciful. One of the most powerful ways to spread that gospel is by living a gracious, loving, forgiving, and merciful life. That's why it's so incredibly important that followers of Christ act like Christ. God has put His reputation on the line through us, through the church. We are to be the "aroma" of Christ, the letters of Christ to the world (2 Corinthians 2:14-16; 3:3).

God will allow evil to do its worst at the very end in order to demonstrate once and for all the huge contrast between being in God's kingdom or in Satan's kingdom. And enduring evil and persecution, resisting them, works to purify the church, strengthening its faith and courage. Churches have experienced explosive growth during difficult times (as in Vietnam and China right now).

So the great-controversy/character-of-God theme ties together all the other threads and gives a clear, cohesive explanation of what God is waiting for. Jesus is a lover. He aches to come. He longs for the moment when He can fulfill that famous promise: "If I go to prepare a place for you, I will come back and take you to be with me that you also may be where I am" (John 14:3). He will come the first moment that all the conditions have been met—when the truth is clear and people have made their choices. That moment is all He has thought about since Satan, the deceiver, told the first lie thousands of years ago.

Last-Day Events and the Book of Revelation

THE BOOK OF REVELATION

Now we will take a brief turn through the incredible, powerful book of Revelation, but asking only one central question—how does it relate to the character of God? First, a few guiding principles I've hammered out for myself:

1. Jesus Christ: This book is first of all the revelation of Jesus Christ (Revelation 1:1). It is from Him, and it is about Him. Therefore, all our interpretation of it must be Christ-centered.

2. Salvation history: Revelation focuses on salvation history, not secular history. It focuses on developments in the great controversy, not secular events. Its central theme is the cosmic battle between good and evil rather than battles between the nations of the world. The church is another major theme of Revelation. God intended this book to convert, to lead to faith, to encourage believers, and to inspire to worship; He didn't mean it to give the inside scoop to an elite group of readers. While making charts based on its contents may serve a purpose, "making" worship and converts takes priority!

3. Themes: Many people avoid Revelation because of the sheer challenge of interpreting all its symbols. However, its broad themes are clear—it is a revelation, after all! It's filled with rich theology and worship, and we shouldn't avoid it because of what we can't master.

4. Multiple applications: The book has multiple applications. It certainly had a primary relevance to the seven churches to which it was originally addressed. It has also been meaningful to each generation as they interpreted its assurances and warnings in light of their own experiences and situation. But it seems obvious that the book is particularly for the last-day generation, whenever that should come. It is like a test-scoring template—the kind with holes that reveal when the students have marked the correct answers. When that template is placed over various eras in history, some of the holes will be filled— and the current generation sees itself in the text and is sure that their times are the final fulfillment of Bible prophecy! But I would suggest that the template will only be completely fulfilled during the last generation immediately before Christ comes.

Therefore, while accepting and affirming the traditional historicist interpretation that Revelation's seven churches, seven seals, and seven trumpets were prophecies that depicted eras of church history over the past two thousand years, the most relevant interpretations concern the final days of earth's history. This is not to defend any traditional futurist interpretation, but simply to say that Revelation has multiple applications, as many other biblical prophecies have had, and the fact that its central focus is on the Second Coming supports looking for an interpretation that keys on the last generation. Since it is a book for the last days, its message will become increasingly clear as the last days draw closer.

5. *Natural reading:* The default method of interpreting Revelation should be the most simple and natural—the way the average reader in any church of any generation would most likely have read it. God does not skew His revelation so far in favor of theologians that the average reader must depend on others to understand it. Scholars are certainly hugely helpful in bringing their knowledge to bear on deeper interpretations, but the natural reading is where we must start. Also, we take passages literally if they make eminent sense as they read and only move to symbolic interpretations if the literal makes no sense or if the context is clearly symbolic.

6. *Chronology:* Revelation should be read and interpreted primarily chronologically. Rather than having the primary/default interpretation include much repeating, reversing, and inverting or using chiastic structures (ABCDDCBA) to interpret the book, we should read it straight through. We should start with the hypothesis that the messages to the seven churches prepare the church for the sealing, which leads us to the warning trumpets, which leads to the final showdown, which leads to the close of probation, which leads to the seven plagues, which leads to the final battle, which leads to the final

victory, the wedding supper of the Lamb, the millennium, and the creation of the new earth. There certainly is room for other, more intricate interpretations—apocalyptic literature can certainly be multilayered—but we start with the straight-forward, natural reading, assuming that the chronology of events roughly follows the sequence in the book, unless forced to adjust.

7. Beasts and dragons: While beasts and dragons can be terrifying, especially as evangelistic artists have often depicted them, they are a part of inspired Scripture, and we must ask what purpose they serve. Here's an illustration: If it could be shown definitively that the CIA and FBI knew about the terrorists' attacks on the World Trade Center before September 11 but failed to warn the public or the airlines or other agencies that could have prevented the loss of thousands of lives—would they not be liable for massive blame? If I were one of those who lost a loved one, and then I met the director of the CIA, I'd have to ask with deep passion, "You knew? You knew all along? How could you know and not warn the rest of us?"

If God knew the identity of the spiritual terrorist powers of the world and failed to warn the unsuspecting world, wouldn't He be partly to blame for the consequences? And if He's going to warn the world, wouldn't beasts and dragons be the best way to reveal the true character of the antichrist powers? When we look at it that way, the beasts and dragons are part of the good news—God is warning us about the incredible powers arrayed against good. Beyond that, it's also clear that God's power far outstrips that of the beasts and Babylons and little horns lined up against Him, and the final outcome is not in doubt!

INTERPRETATION OF REVELATION

If these assumptions are legitimate, we can attempt a broad outline of the flow of Revelation:

Seven churches: The messages to the seven churches, while having an initial relevance to the first-century churches and also representing eras of church history, have their *major* impact in preparing the last-day church to give the final message to the world—preparing it to be sealed and ready for the final events. The remnant church that is the final witness to the world will be a composite of the best traits of all seven churches—loving, faithful, uncompromising, alive, and white-hot.

Seven seals/seven trumpets/seven plagues: While acknowledging the value of the historicist interpretation of the seals and the trumpets, taking a multilayered approach allows us to focus on the central thrust of Revelation, which is to prepare people for the final showdown at the end of the world. Surely there is an application for our contemporary generation of the first half of the book beyond a history lesson about the past two thousand years!

In Revelation 7, the angels are told not to harm nature until the special group has been sealed. But the seven trumpets promptly *do* harm nature—implying that the sealing has begun. There's also a very interesting progression: Under the seals it is stated that one-fourth of earth's citizens will be destroyed; under the trumpets, one-third is destroyed; and under the plagues, God's "wrath" is poured out "full strength" (Revelation 6:8; 8:7, 9, 11, 12; 14:10).

Progressive evil: Reading Revelation from the perspective of our great-controversy understanding of the issues in the final showdown, we realize that God has allowed Satan a great deal of leeway to do his worst while he tries to draw people away from God (see Job 1). But Revelation 7 indicates that God has had angels intervening, holding back the winds of strife, or it would have been much worse. However, as the final showdown approaches, God allows Satan to do his very worst. The entire universe needs to see what life would look like under Satan's unimpeded control. It's the only way the "election" can be fair. And it is the only way that the righteous will be convinced forever of the stupidity and disaster of ever reverting back to sin.

God withdraws His intervening power in stages so that first one-fourth is destroyed, then one-third, and then there is total devastation. These fractions represent partial destruction and show the expanding concentric circles of the consequences of evil. This is also what it means to live "without an intercessor." This phrase certainly cannot mean that we no longer have access to grace or to the intercession of Christ (Philippians 3:8-10; Hebrews 7:25). God's people will forever have to rely on grace, and Christ will forever be the "open door" to the truth about God's grace (Revelation 3:8; Hebrews 4:16).[5]

THE KING'S ELECTION

Here's a parable that illustrates why God allows evil to expand its role: Once upon a time there was a country with a wonderful king. He loved his people and took care of them. All the citizens were rich and healthy, and they had wonderful lives.

Eventually, though, the people looked around at the countries where the citizens elected their own presidents. The people of the kingdom staged a coup, sending the king into retirement in the country, and elected his son as president. But the son wasn't like his father. He ruined the country's economy and taxed the people until they were poor and starving. Soon total chaos prevailed: The rate of inflation reached 1,000 percent, there was no food in the stores or medicine in the hospitals, and the country was overrun with illegal drugs and crime.

The king heard about what was happening. Quietly he began to send his own money to people anonymously. He sent medicine to the hospitals to keep people alive and food into the markets. He paid off the countries around so they wouldn't invade his country. But the king's son took credit for all the good the king was doing, saying he was supplying the money.

Eventually, the situation became so bad that the king's aides told him that if the country were to be saved, he must run against his son in the next election.

"I can't do it," the king said.

"You have to. It's the only hope for the country," his aides replied.

Finally he did it. He put his name in and began to run. But it wasn't easy. He held press conferences, but almost no one came. He planned big rallies with music and speeches, but just a few old people who remembered him turned out.

His aides told him, "You're going to have to let people know that you're the one who's keeping everybody alive."

So he began to let his aides go on *Meet the Press* and *60 Minutes* to tell the truth about what was happening. They said the son had stolen billions from the country. And they said that it was really the king who was sending money to the poor, medicine to the hospitals, food to the stores, and keeping their enemies from invading the country. They said the king had governed the country better than the son was running it now. But very few believed them.

Finally, the aides met with the king. They told him, "You are going to have to—just for a short time—let people see what it would really be like under your son."

"I can't do that," the king replied. "Think what would happen—how people would suffer!"

"We know," the aides said. "But it's the only way they'll ever learn the truth. Once you become king again, you can end the suffering forever."

The king agonized. He paced the halls at night, crying, trying to find some other way to save the country. But finally he told them to do it, but to do it gradually, hoping that everyone would realize the truth quickly. So the first week they reduced the payments, food, and medicine a little. The next week they cut back some more. Some began to realize that the king had been telling the truth and began to come to the king's rallies. The aides cut back more, and more people began to come to the rallies, desperate for a change, desperate to bring back the former king. The rallies became exciting: Thousands were coming and cheering and singing his praise.

The polls showed that the king was gaining every week, but the election was still in doubt. So the king withdrew all the payments, all the help—leaving the country totally in the control of the evil son. Now they would know *exactly* what life would be like if the king were totally out of the way and the country completely at the mercy of his son. People were starving, dying for lack of medicine; there were funerals every day. The king watched it all on television. Tears streamed down his cheeks. The people's suffering hurt him deeply.

Finally the election came, and everyone had a choice: the son or the former king. The king watched as the votes were counted. Finally, at midnight, he was declared the winner. Millions streamed into the streets for a huge party. The king was back! The whole country rocked with music and dancing in the streets. The citizens took over the palace, threw the son out, and carried the king back in.

The king began to send money to all who wanted it—and food and medicine and everything else they needed. Those who had voted for the son refused to take any of it, and soon they were gone. It wasn't long until the only ones left in the country were those who had voted for the king, who loved the king. He restored their prosperity and happiness, and the music played and the people danced forever and forever!

For heaven and the new earth to be both safe and free, God has to make sure that everyone has become convinced once and for all that no better alternative to God exists. The conviction that sin kills must be burned indelibly in people's minds.

To summarize: (1) The messages to the seven churches will be preached with power, preparing a remnant people to share with the world the truth about God. They will all have a first-love, white-hot relationship with God. This group will begin to be sealed and begin to share the final message about God with latter-rain power. (2) Then the seven seals will be poured out, demonstrating with increased severity the consequences of evil. (3) Next, the seven trumpets will play. No one will ever be able to remonstrate with God, asking, "Why didn't You make it clearer?" God announces the final demonstration of evil "with trumpets." No one will sleep through this!

FINAL SHOWDOWN!

This all leads to the final showdown: Revelation 12-14. These chapters introduce the key players of the final drama symbolically, with God, Christ, and the church on one side and the dragon and the sea and land beasts on the other. The final showdown is the ultimate, fourth-quarter, pivotal clash between two ideologies, two philosophies, two versions of "truth." One side is willing to use any "weapon" to win; the other side will use only those "weapons" consistent with God's character—truth, love, goodness, gentleness, evidence.

All the while that evil is progressing and having its way all over the world, God is empowering a group of people to lift Him up in a way the world has never seen before. The 144,000* witness to the truth about God under the power of the Holy Spirit and the latter rain. They preach the three angels' messages of Revelation 14:6-12. The truth about God will spread like wildfire around the world. It will be on the Internet. People will be discussing it on all the talk shows. Seekers will fill stadiums, coming to hear what they've been missing all their lives. It will be an exciting time!

Some believe the last days will be a time of trouble that they would prefer to sleep through, waking up just in time to see Christ coming on the clouds. Not me! I've been waiting all my life to see the day when stadiums will be full of people wanting to get God right, to know God exactly the way He is, free of the distortions and caricatures that have accumulated even in the Christian church. I don't want to sleep through it all!

When I was in the seminary, my brother Donald sent me tickets to a Chicago Bulls-Portland Trailblazers basketball game in Chicago.

---

*144,000 is a symbolic number that represents God's last-day people who will give the clearest witness about Him to the world—see chapter 13.

Last-Day Events and the Book of Revelation

Both teams were good; the Trailblazers were the world champions at the time. I invited a friend to come with me. Before attending the seminary, I'd been a youth pastor in Portland, so my friend and I would stand and cheer whenever the Trailblazers scored. Of course, twenty thousand Chicagoans would stand and cheer whenever the Bulls scored!

Near the end of the game, one of the Bulls stole the ball, dribbled it down the court, and dunked it, putting his team ahead by one point—and twenty thousand fans stood and cheered! The Trailblazers immediately called time out, but there were just four seconds left till the final buzzer. One of the Trailblazers inbounded the ball, and Lionel Hollins caught the pass and threw a long shot. The ball banked into the basket as the buzzer went off—and the Trailblazers won by one point! And so two of us were standing and cheering while twenty thousand sat stark silent. Someone sitting behind us tapped me on the shoulder and said, "You've been waiting the whole game for that, haven't you!" Maybe that is what David was talking about when he said, "Thou preparest a table before me in the presence of mine enemies" (Psalm 23:5, KJV)!

At times it may look to us as if the other side is going win, that maybe we joined the wrong team. But I believe that the time is coming when God will come through, and we'll be cheering while the rest of the world goes silent. Don't miss it!

Close of probation: When the final showdown comes to a head and the issues are crystal clear and everyone alive in the world has had a quality chance to make an informed, voluntary decision for or against God, probation will close. God will not sneak the close of probation up on anyone. He won't close probation until He knows, in His omniscient wisdom, that everyone has made an irrevocable, final decision one way or the other. He is never arbitrary!

At that point there's no reason to delay any longer. The time for which God has been waiting for thousands of years will have finally arrived. Everything is settled. The questions have all been answered. He's found a way to justify people without compromising His justice (Romans 3:24-26). Why wait any longer? God is a lover, waiting to get married. And so all of heaven leaves the temple, and begins the descent to earth to gather all of God's friends (Matthew 24:31; Revelation 15). Many of us believe that the "silence in heaven" (Revelation 8:1) is a symbol of the fact that heaven is empty—everyone has left to come get the saints and bring them home!

Seven last plagues: The plagues then fall on those who have the mark of the beast. No one receives the mark of the beast until they've been sealed after the close of probation, which is why I believe, along with many others, that the plagues fall after the close of probation (Revelation 15, 16).

Who sends the plagues? This is one of the challenging questions regarding God's character. There are two main points of view. One says God is certainly loving, merciful, and forgiving, but He is also committed to justice. Justice demands that these people who have caused unspeakable suffering should endure some sort of punishment before they die. The cries of suffering people, oppressed by beasts and Babylons, have gone up to God for thousands of years. Their cries have broken His heart as He has had to stand aside and watch. So, in this view, the plagues are God's assurance that all injustice and pain will end. God will square everything up; justice will be done; "vengeance is mine saith the Lord."

The other view has been the theme of this book. It says that God is not like that. He is gracious and loving and life-giving. The progression of the seals (one-fourth), trumpets (one-third), and the plagues (unmixed with mercy) seems to indicate that all three of these "judgments" are from the side of evil; God has reluctantly allowed them to occur as part of His commitment to making the universe safe. God has to ensure that people have learned the laws of cause and effect once and for all through seeing the devastation that results when sin is allowed full sway.

Last-Day Events and the Book of Revelation

This is the view that Ellen White seems to support in *The Great Controversy*:

> The restraint . . . upon the wicked is removed, and Satan has entire control of the finally impenitent. . . . The Spirit of God . . . has been at last withdrawn. Unsheltered by divine grace, they [the unrepentant] have no protection from the wicked one. Satan will then plunge the inhabitants of the earth into one great, final trouble. As the angels of God cease to hold in check the fierce winds of human passion, all the elements of strife will be let loose.[6]

I believe that this time of trouble will be very short. Prolonging suffering would serve no purpose. Once the point is made, God wants to redeem His people and take them home. He's been waiting for a long time, and He won't wait one second longer than absolutely necessary.

Second coming: Imagine what Christ's second coming will be like! During the days just before the start of the new millennium, I happened to see some show that ranked the top twenty-five music videos. The most popular was *Thriller* by Michael Jackson—something I'd never seen. In one scene, set in a cemetery, the headstones began to move and shake, and then horrible, bony hands came out. Pretty soon all these ghouls came out of their graves and went dancing down the street with Michael Jackson. What a horrible, sacrilegious mockery of what will be, for many of us, one of the greatest events in history!

When I was in college, my grandfather Dan Venden took a whole group of my generation of the family to see the graves of his parents, who more than a hundred years ago became the first Adventists in the family. My grandfather said, with tears streaming down his face, "One of these days these stones will go tumbling down the hill." It's going to happen.

The wicked will all die the first death, and the righteous will all be swept up into the clouds. All the righteous of all the centuries from all over the world will be together for the first time. During the next thousand years, we'll become "community." We'll be healed of all the results of sin. Some people will never have heard the name of Christ—but they've been friends of God, and the moment they meet Christ, they'll love and embrace Him, because He's even better than the picture of God they'd already embraced.

Millennium: The investigative judgment (the first judgment), which we discussed in chapter 8, will have been completed. The universe will have seen that God's decisions as to whom to save have been absolutely just (Daniel 8:14; Romans 3:24-26; Revelation 15:3, 4). During the millennium, the saints also will judge. (See Revelation 20:4-6; this is the second judgment.) I understand this to mean that during that time the righteous will ask all the questions that may still be lurking in their minds. Why are some in heaven whom they didn't expect to see there? Why are others not there? Could more have been done to save them? Could God have handled some situations more aggressively? God will throw open the "books," every question will be answered, and all will bow and acknowledge God as absolutely righteous (Daniel 9:14; Revelation 15:3, 4; Philippians 2:9-11).

People have asked me, "Won't it hurt to look at the books, to read the history of this world? I thought that after Jesus comes, there won't be any pain or tears."

God promised no more tears in the new earth. But during the thousand years, we may well have a few hard moments. How could we not? It will hurt, yes. We'll miss some people. That will be heartbreaking to God as well. But we'll have a thousand years to be healed, to become a community that will spend forever together.

Then comes the great white throne judgment of Revelation 20:11-15 (judgment number three). All the wicked will be raised to life again after "sleeping" for a thousand years (the first death). That "looses" Satan to deceive the nations again. The New Jerusalem has descended. Satan and all those on his side circle the city and rush to destroy God and all the righteous, demonstrating that their essential character hasn't changed whatsoever—in case anyone wonders what would have happened if they'd been given "one more chance."

The Spirit of Prophecy indicates that at that time, God has one final demonstration to make. Perhaps on something like a huge video screen, He'll review the major events of salvation history. Most of us will see these events for the first time, in such vividness that we'll feel as though we *were* there the first time. We'll see the Cross and the resurrection. Every being in the entire universe will see all that they need to see, until all are convinced that God has been telling the absolute truth all along.

The righteous will bow and lay their crowns at Christ's feet. The wicked will also bow at His feet. And we're told that, finally, even Satan will bow and acknowledge—voluntarily, but maybe through clenched teeth—Christ's supremacy and righteousness. At that moment every being will have acknowledged that God is right and Lucifer is wrong. And the righteous will remember forever that the wicked themselves acknowledged the truth about God before they died.

New earth: After all the wicked are dead, the Fire will cleanse every trace of sin from the earth, and God will create the new earth. Then the grand plan will be complete. The universe will be safe. No pockets of hell will exist where people are screaming and cursing in pain. All traces of sin will be gone. God will dwell with us. He will be our God, and we will be His people—forever.

Could it ever all happen again? No. Scripture says sin will not arise a second time (Nahum 1:9). God has gone to great lengths to answer every question. Everyone will have seen and heard the truth about God through the story of Christ, through the Bible, and through the final witnesses. They will have seen the graphic reality of God's first warning message: If you eat of the Tree, you will surely die. They will have touched the stove and found that it burns. They understand fire law.

The moment people walk through the gates of heaven, they'll experience down to the depths of their soul the healing power of the love of God—they'll feel it face to face in a way we get only a taste of down here. Their soul was made for God. Sin was just an attempt to fill the void left when they had no personal relationship with God. Now the pure, unmediated love of God fills that void.

We sin because we want certain needs met. Now all those needs are totally met, forever. We'll have mansions. We'll eat from the Tree of life. Jesus said we'd never hunger and thirst again, and we won't. We'll never be bored, never covet, never steal, never be jealous. We'll be satisfied—forever.

When Satan and the demons are gone, we'll experience only love and grace and worship and service, everywhere. Our bodies will have been changed from mortal to immortal. We'll all be like Christ, exactly as we were created to be. That's why sin will never happen again. Forever.

The end is best described by the last paragraph of one of the best books on the last days, *The Great Controversy Between Christ and Satan:*

> The great controversy is ended. Sin and sinners are no more. The entire universe is clean. One pulse of harmony and gladness beats through the vast creation. From Him who created all, flow life and light and gladness, throughout the realms of illimitable space. From the minutest atom to the greatest world, all things, animate and inanimate, in their unshadowed beauty and perfect joy, declare that God is love.[7]

---

1. Lewis, *The Four Loves*, 190, 191.

2. White, *Christ's Object Lessons*, 69.

3. White, *Review and Herald*, August 17, 1901.

4. White, *Christ's Object Lessons*, 415, 416.

5. See Morris Venden, *Never Without An Intercessor: The Good News About the Judgment* (Nampa, Idaho: Pacific Press, 1996).

6. White, *Great Controversy*, 614.

7. Ibid., 678.

CHAPTER THIRTEEN

Impact Players

I heard a terrific sermon by Bill Hybels one Friday night. He was speaking over Moody Radio to hundreds of young people for Founders Week. He said that God was looking for impact players. Coaches of athletic teams look for impact players—players who are not satisfied just to sit on the bench or to be role players on a team. When the game is on the line they want the ball. They aren't afraid to take the final shot. Michael Jordan, Magic Johnson, Joe Montana—they were impact players.

And it's not just in sports. William Wilberforce. Gandhi. Martin Luther King, Jr. Nelson Mandela. Mother Teresa. All of them were impact players—people who refused to accept the status quo; people who were willing to pour out their lives to make a difference in the world, who couldn't accept standing on the sidelines. People who knew they had only one life to live and wanted to live it to the max.

Hybels said that God is looking for impact players who will make an eternal impact on the world. That's what I want to say in this last chapter: God is looking for impact players. People who can't bear to hear God's character compromised in any way. People who are as willing to plant the flag of the truth about God as those six soldiers who raised the U.S. flag on Iwo Jima. People like the three mighty men who broke through enemy lines to get a cup of water for David.

People like Daniel's three friends, who stood when everyone else bowed down to the image. People like Daniel himself, who could walk into Belshazzar's party and interpret the handwriting on the wall to a thousand men who'd been drinking from the holy vessels of the temple in Jerusalem.

We are being called to walk boldly into the halls and hallways of the world and interpret the handwriting on the wall for the world, to interpret the mysteries of the truth about God. What an incredible honor! I've heard that after Muhammad Ali was chosen to carry the Olympic flame up the steps to begin the Atlanta Games, he sat for hours holding the torch, reveling in the honor of having been chosen out of all the American athletes. It's an even greater honor to hold God's reputation in our hands!

THE 144,000 QUESTION

There's been a huge debate over who comprise the 144,000 mentioned in Revelation 7:14.[1] A growing number of us have wondered if this group is a symbol* that represents those who will give a witness to the world just before Christ comes. They are the first to be sealed, who then give the three angels' messages to the world with latter-rain power.

Why? Revelation 12-14 covers the final showdown. Revelation 14:1-5, which describes the 144,000, is followed by Revelation 14:6-12, the three angels' messages, followed by Revelation 14:13ff, the Second-Coming harvest. It seems logical that the 144,000 are the group who give the final messages in the showdown.

What are their traits? (1) They have the names of God and the Son on their foreheads (Revelation 14:1). God's name stands for His

---

*A symbol because (1) spiritual Israel has replaced literal Israel (Romans 9-11; Galatians 3:16, 29; 6:15); (2) the tribal distinctions have been erased; (3) the exact twelve thousand from each tribe seems symbolic; (4) the numerical factors—$12^2 \times 10^3$—clearly are significant biblical numbers; (5) and they are all men and virgins (Revelation 14:4, 5).

character; these people would rather die than do anything that would dishonor or misrepresent God in any way.

(2) These people have assurance. They are pictured as standing on the heavenly Mount Zion, while the context clearly shows that they are still down here on earth. But they are so firmly sealed into Christ that they are regarded as if they're already in heaven.[2]

(3) They refuse to defile themselves with women—meaning that they're absolutely monogamous in their marriage with God (Revelation 14:4; cp. Song of Solomon, Hosea, Revelation 19). They refuse to have any other gods. They hate sin (see also Genesis 3:15).

(4) They're the "firstfruits of God and the Lamb" (Revelation 14:4). They're the first to be sealed, after which they go out to preach the final message, bringing millions of others to salvation.

(5) They "follow the Lamb wherever He goes" (Revelation 14:4). The best way to avoid debating perfection is simply to put it in a relational context: The 144,000 will follow the Lamb wherever He goes. If they're with Christ wherever He goes, they'll get where they need to be! They have the fullness of the best of the traits the messages to the seven churches describe; they're in their first-love experience spiritually, uncompromising, alive, and open to and white-hot for God!

(6) "No lie was found in their mouths" (Revelation 14:5). They refuse to accept a single one of Satan's lies about God. Their passion is to speak and live only the absolute truth about God.

Acts 2 describes two groups that perhaps parallel the 144,000 and the great multitude of Revelation 7. The first group are the disciples in the upper room, who've been intimately connected with Christ and who are so deeply committed that all of them are willing even to be martyrs for Christ. They've been praying, they're united, they're experiencing true community, and they're filled with the Holy Spirit. They're on fire! They go out to preach to the massive crowd, and three thousand are converted in a day.

Could it be that the 144,000, who have been with Christ, who are sealed into Christ, who are white-hot for God, and who go out and give the final witness for Christ, parallels this upper-room group and that the great multitude whom "no man could number" that will come to salvation during that final witness parallels the three thousand? It's possible!

OUR ROLE—IMPACT PLAYERS

What's our role, then, as a church? We're to be a part of that group of impact players! Centuries of accumulated dust and grime hid the true, jaw-dropping beauty of the Sistine Chapel. Art restorers had to work for years to reveal the full impact of Michelangelo's art. That is what we do for God; we scrape away the distortions about the character of God that have accumulated for centuries and restore the truth about God for the world to see in all its beauty.

Once when my brothers and I went to a Los Angeles Lakers game, we were seated in the very last, highest row, so far from the court that we couldn't identify the players. But toward the end of the game, as people began to leave, we moved down to their seats closer to the court. We ended up practically at courtside and were shocked to see how much bigger and faster the players appeared to be from that perspective! As a church we are the ushers, inviting people to "come on down" to see God as incredibly more awesome than they could ever have imagined before.

In the movie *Twelve Angry Men*, Henry Fonda is the lone juror who votes to acquit the defendant. By the end of the story he has argued and challenged and presented the evidence until finally he has persuaded all the others to vote "not guilty." That's what we'll do for God, until the entire universe votes "not guilty."

In Revelation 4 and 5, John says he saw an open door into the throne room of heaven. He sees Someone on the throne who is holding a scroll sealed with seven seals. But John begins to weep because no one is worthy to open the scrolls. Then one of the elders points to a Lamb, a symbol of Christ, who is worthy to open the scroll (Revelation 5:6, 7).

What does the scroll contain? Christ is the only One worthy to open it—and what is the one thing that only Christ has been able to do? Tell the truth about God. "No one has ever seen God, but God the One and Only, who is at the Father's side, has made him known" (John 1:18; see also Hebrews 1:1-3). I believe that the scroll is the story of the questions that we've been studying—the questions about God that Satan has been asking for thousands of years, and Christ's answers to Satan's charges.

Revelation 4 and 5 contain five hymns. With each hymn the choir becomes larger. First, the *four living creatures* sing, "Holy, holy, holy" (Revelation 4:6-8). Next, the *twenty-four elders* sing (Revelation 4:11). Then the *twenty-four and the four* sing, "You are worthy . . . because you were slain, and with your blood you purchased men for God" (Revelation 5:9, 10). They're followed by all the *angels,** and then, finally, *every creature* sings (Revelation 5:11, 12; verse 13).†

The time is coming when every single being who has ever lived will be alive at the very same time, and every single one of them will be singing in this choir. As Paul says, every knee will bow and every tongue will confess that Jesus is Lord (Philippians 2:10, 11). Like Daniel, every being will say, "The LORD is righteous in all that He does" (Daniel 9:14). We're told that eventually even Satan himself will bow and admit that God is righteous.[3] While other events follow, in a sense Satan's voluntary admission that he was wrong and that God was right is the culmination of the great controversy. All

---

*Christ died even for the sinless angels, to answer their questions (Colossians 1:19, 20).

†Notice the concentric squares—the squared numbers: four (one per side); twenty-four (six per side); twenty-eight (seven per side); and ten thousand times ten thousand (twenty-five million per side). Most likely they comprise a terrific symbol of the completeness of God's kingdom, a perfect square.

Satan's claims to the contrary were lies. God was and is righteous and loving and gracious. He couldn't have been any better. And the entire universe sings, "To him who sits on the throne and to the Lamb be praise and honor and glory and power, for ever and ever!" (Revelation 5:13) What a moment!

Years ago, while I was pastoring in Hinsdale, Illinois, three young men in their twenties flew up to Wisconsin to ski. A storm arose, and their plane crashed, killing all three. I drove to Andrews University to help Dwight Nelson with the funeral for one of the young men, who was an only child. His parents asked Dr. Warren Becker, the organist of the Pioneer Memorial Church on the Andrews University campus, to play the hymn "Guide Me, O Thou Great Jehovah" on the great pipe organ during the funeral.

Dr. Becker played the first verse as it appears in the hymnal. With the second verse, he began to add more pipes, some variations. With the third verse, he was all over that organ, and thousands of pipes were throbbing with sound; I could feel it all coming through the platform floor. By the fourth verse, that grand church was rocking with sound!

ADDING VOICES TO THE CHOIR

I think that's how these songs in Revelation 4 and 5 will grow. They start with the four living creatures thousands of years ago, right after Lucifer's apostasy. They swelled to the twenty-four, then the twenty-eight, then to all the angels—and finally the grand chorus of the entire universe. Someday all creation is going to rock with worship honoring God. That will be the ultimate fulfillment of Daniel 8:14, "Then the sanctuary shall be restored to its rightful state." That will be Yom Kippur.

Think what that moment will mean to God. He's had to offer up His Son. He's had to wait through thousands of years of having His character denigrated, of sitting by while people He loved were forced to endure heartbreaking suffering. But this night it's all over. Everything has been made right. And the eternal party to end all parties can begin!

If this is true and this is what we are waiting for, then what is the one thing we can do? We can add our voices to the choir! When we tell the truth about God, we add another voice to the choir. When we raise a child who knows God as *only* gracious and loving, we add another voice to the choir. Each Sabbath School lesson, each worship, each mission trip, each dollar given brings that moment closer. That is why we need impact players!

Think what that first worship service will be like when earth's troubles are all over. The wicked are gone forever. Satan and his demons are no more. And millions who all love God will come to worship. Imagine the music!

But the moment to end all moments will be when Christ stands up and introduces the Father. We'll give Him a standing ovation. Then Christ will gesture for silence. In a voice choked with emotion, He'll say to the Father, "They're all here. I died for them. They're back. They're home. They're Yours—forever." And He'll give the church to the Father. It's His gift from the Cross. This is what He died to accomplish—"the joy set before him" for which He "endured the cross, scorning its shame" (Hebrews 12:2).

No other moment can match that one! Every moment of joy down here is just a taste of what we will feel there, in the presence of God, forever. We will "sup with Him, and He with us" every day, forever.

And as the song says, "forever is a long, long time!"

---

1. In *Selected Messages*, 1:174, Mrs. White counsels us to avoid controversy over who will comprise this group.

2. Beatrice Neall, "Sealed Saints and the Tribulation," *Symposium on Revelation*, Frank B. Holbrook, ed. (Hagerstown, Md.: Review and Herald, 1992), 1:270-272.

3. White, *Great Controversy*, 670.

Appendix

STAGES OF MORAL DEVELOPMENT

Here is a summary of Lawrence Kohlberg's six stages of moral development:

Stage One: Avoid Punishment. We obey rules to avoid punishment. (Think of babies, who know only that they should stop doing whatever gives them pain.) Our definition of what is wrong is whatever gets punished.

Stage Two: Rewards. We do whatever will be rewarded, whether that reward is ice cream or a star from the piano teacher or a school ski trip. What is right is what gets rewarded.

Stage Three: Social Approval. We evaluate behavior by other people's opinions. My mother would never let my father grow a beard even while they were touring China. "We might bump into some Adventists, and what will they think?" We are not sincerely motivated by what is really right or wrong but by what people will think.

Stage Four: Law and Order. We conform our actions to authority, whether that authority is our parents, our teachers, our boss, the government, or even God. We don't make the laws, and we may not even think they make sense, but "it's the law," and it's less hassle to just obey. We haven't really bought into the concept or accepted the cause-and-effect nature of natural consequences. We don't wear seatbelts because of safety but because we don't want to get a ticket. We don't learn for the love and power of learning but in order to get grades, to keep people happy, etc.

Note: All the motivations in stages one through four are external. We do the right thing and avoid evil because of what someone outside of us might do or think: our parents, teachers, boss, coach, government, or even God. Stages five and six are more internally motivated.

Stage Five: Necessary for the Public Good. We begin to understand what is necessary for the public good. We understand that we need to drive on our side of the road so all the people who are traveling can get where they're going quickly and safely. We understand that no one wins a nuclear war.

Stage Six: Personalized Ethical Principles. We live by self-chosen, internalized ethical principles, such as love, equality, authenticity, truthfulness, courtesy, the Golden Rule, etc. The law is now written on our hearts, and it is natural, instinctive. We do what is right because it is right, because it makes sense—no matter who is or isn't around, what time of day it is, how far we are from home, or what the consequences are.

Index

Index

If you enjoyed this book, you'll enjoy these as well:

Journey to Moriah

Ken Wade invites us to go on a spiritual adventure with Abraham—seeing life through his eyes, entering into his culture, and learning with him how to really walk with God. Along the way, Wade shows us a new picture of the "friend of God." We see a real human being with faults and flaws that needed to be smoothed over. And we see a man steeped in pagan culture trying to learn the ways of Jehovah.

0-8163-2024-1. Paperback.
US$11.99, Can$17.99.

Wonderful Words of Life

Morris Venden. Known for his ability to apply parables to the Christian experience, pastor and author Morris Venden gives us new pictures of grace in some of Jesus's most unusual stories. This book unravels the mysteries wrapped up in the "problem" parables and exposes the Master story teller's strategy for victorious Christian living.

0-8163-2008-X. Paperback.
US$12.99, Can$19.49.

Living in the Light

Douglas Cooper, best known for his classic *Living God's Love,* is back to show what can happen when ordinary people embrace and are indwelled by an extraordinary God. *Living in the Light* takes us on a journey beyond codes, tradition, and religiosity to the power of personal, genuine spirituality—living constantly in an attitude of love and forgiveness.

0-8163-2015-2. Paperback.
US$10.99,Can$16.49.

Order from your ABC by calling **1-800-765-6955**, or get online and shop our virtual store at **www.AdventistBookCenter.com**.
- Read a chapter from your favorite book
- Order online
- Sign up for email notices on new products

Prices subject to change without notice.